Exit Strategy

Exit Strategy

Ending the Tyranny of Finance

Giulio Tremonti

Rizzoli
ex libris

First published in the United States of America in 2012 by
Rizzoli Ex Libris
An imprint of Rizzoli International Publications, Inc.
300 Park Avenue South
New York, NY 10010
www.rizzoliusa.com

Translated by Emily Kate Price

Originally published in Italian as *Uscita di sicurezza* in 2012
by RCS Libri S.p.A.

2012 2013 2014 2015 / 10 9 8 7 6 5 4 3 2 1

Distributed in the U.S. trade by Random House, New York

Printed in Italy

ISBN-13: 978-0-8478-4024-3

Library of Congress Catalog Control Number: 2012938806

Contents

Exit Strategy

Introduction

Noah's Ark was built by amateurs. The Titanic was built by professionals.

The former, the ark, is an ancient image of salvation. The latter, the Titanic, is the epitome of disaster in our times.

The first vessel, the fantastical one, worked and still has the capacity to work because it comes to man from his creator spirit, who commanded, "Make yourself an ark of cypress wood."

The second type of vessel, the technically correct one, can work, but it can also fail. And it often does fail if it is made by man and for man only. It fails above all if it is made by the worst part of mankind: the "selfish gene," the matrix of a process whose ideology is a form of social Darwinism applied to economics, proof that *homo homini lupus est,* or man acts as wolf toward his fellow man.

Today, lupine man's ideal hunting ground is the financial market. Due to an extraordinary process of concentration and degeneration in mental, social, judicial and economic structures, the financial market today is seen as the center of the market, which itself is seen as the center of human life. A metaphysical entity, an oracle, with its ritualistic and mysterious dealings, autistic and mathematical, the financial market, positioned as an arcane and almost sacred space, is seemingly able to judge us, save us and damn us, both as peoples and as individuals. The financial market, as it has developed and been organized over the years, can and does do this, and it has been left to do this freely, putting profit before justice, reducing our attention to morality and policy, making old regulatory standards unimportant, zeroing out ethical values and privatizing the law, allowing the few powerful figures who rule the planet to prey unmercifully upon the weak, replacing empathy with selfishness, dismissing the idea that we survive precisely because we are socially-minded creatures and not the opposite and, ultimately, taking us from order to chaos.

The financial market's potent dominant ideology tends to exclude the best aspects of human nature, reducing life to economics and economics to finance. Thus it becomes a monster that today feeds on us and later will feed on itself.

A few true believers attempt to humanize this monster in order to make it approachable. They create an anthropomorphic image of it, speaking in hushed tones, for example, of "market sentiment."

This is all very far from Adam Smith's market bible,

The Wealth of Nations, a study of the nature and causes of that wealth.

Wealth matters, but so do nations. For centuries they have anchored the civic values of their communities. Those values historically were based on moral responsibility and political structures. However, today's wealth is slowly on its way to destroying these nations, and it will in the end destroy itself, too. This dual destruction will be as much political as it is economic.

This destructive process and its ongoing development will be illustrated in the pages that follow. You will also find a summary of it in the diagrams beginning on page 49—diagrams that clearly and undeniably demonstrate how a new form of capitalism has developed over the last twenty years. That new form of capitalism developed on the backs of globalization and then via the Internet. This is not, as Marx would have it, a capitalism stuck in dialectic and torn by the conflict between constant capital and variable capital, the former consisting of the means of production and goods and circulating capital, and the latter of the workforce. This is something else. Unexpectedly, at this time in history, the original financial core of circulating capital has evolved and expanded naturally through globalization and the Internet. It has steadily accumulated so much force that a completely new type of capital has resulted: dominant capital, the basis of the transnational superpower of the financial market. In its current form, it expresses and establishes the modern dictatorship of money.

This form of capitalism, dominant as it is, is also dying. The fiction underlying it cannot survive. And its basis is clearly fiction, as shown in the formula—which resembles hieroglyphics—on page 63. This process may have been developed on the industrial and global scale that is now typical of techno-finance, but it is not far removed from the mad and fatal bargain between Faust and Mephistopheles.

Why and how did this degenerative and destructive process develop? Through what types of mechanisms—physical, political, material, mental, real or symbolic, ethological or practical? And what can be done to stop it?

One thing is certain: The crisis we're currently experiencing did not come from nowhere. It hasn't happened by chance. It was not caused by an obscure and unknown nemesis. It is the result of man's actions.

What follows here is a narrative that lies somewhere between memoir and journalism. In these pages are things that I saw and experienced, both during the last five years since the explosion of the financial crisis in the summer of 2007 and before that.

These are reflections and affirmations from international summits and conferences, but from the very beginning I heard them repeated verbatim in many other places: from the Università Cattolica (Milan) to Chatham House (London), from the New World, New Capitalism conference in Paris to the Central School of the Chinese Communist Party in Beijing. I heard them at universities such as Freiburg and Yale and at the Herzliya Conference in Tel Aviv and on many other public occasions. Little of what I said in these places reflects the standard tone of the official communications that are passed around with little fanfare at international summits. Those are traditionally dominated by a non-nationalistic and impersonal centralism. This tone is so pervasive that it excludes the democratic consideration of theories and ideas that differ from prevailing thought. But everything said outside of these summits and written here does truly reflect what was said within them, beginning in 2008, concerning the relationship between states and finance, concerning regulation and a proposed European fund and so on.[1]

In any case, being on the inside helped me better to understand the situation. It's one thing to read articles in the press and official documents, but quite another to see the actions of individuals and forces that have created (or failed to create) the policies.

Finally: this book is in part an affirmation, in the truest sense of the word. Much of what I predicted in my

[1] See Appendix 1, made up of 3 documents: a letter to the then French finance minister, Christine Lagarde (at the time of France's presidency of the European Union); the economic program of the Italian G7/G8 2009 presidency; and a proposal for a European fund. Appendix 2 contains the preface to the Japanese edition of *La paura e la speranza* (The Fear and the Hope), written by the former governor of the Bank of Japan. The first three documents in particular anticipate the conclusions reached in this book on the relationship between the state and finance, on the necessity of new global regulations and on the urgent need for a European fund.

previous book, *La paura e la speranza* (The Fear and the Hope), published in 2008 has come to pass.[2]

And this book is in part a modification of that one, as it discusses things that couldn't have been predicted back then. It was already possible to predict the crisis—the domino-like collapse of the financial pyramids, the global megabanks of Wall Street. However, it was simply impossible to predict when and how the crisis would occur: which day, which bank, what the effects would be, how intense it would be. And it was certainly impossible to predict which policies would be adopted to "manage" it.

I have been searching for an appropriate metaphor to describe this crisis since it began, and I still have not found a better image than that of a series of video-game monsters. You are playing a game, and a monster arrives, so you fight it, and you destroy it. Your impulse is to relax for a moment, but immediately a second monster, bigger than the first, pops up on the screen. And so on. At the end of this book, I will suggest a way for us to escape from this video game.

When in 2006 I predicted there would be "another 1929," it was just a guess.[3] A guess that, sadly, turned out to be true, give or take a few small differences, because history never repeats itself down to the last detail. Yet

[2] The first few pages of this book are contained in Appendix 3.

[3] In the *Corriere della Sera* newspaper November 12, 2006.

after 1929 came 1933, the lowest point of the Great Depression, when the crisis gradually moved from being an artificial, financial one to a real crisis with impact on people's lives. (For better understanding of that period, read *The Grapes of Wrath*, or think of Nazism taking hold in Germany at that time.) That crisis erupted in a society that was still relatively poor, while the current one is taking place in a society that is much more affluent overall, and even extremely wealthy in places. That doesn't make the impact any less risky, or less violent. On the contrary, this crisis has the potential to cause conflicts, social rebellion and protest. Such new political movements could then generate new styles of politics. This has happened in the past and we are beginning to see it again now. When power manipulates the financial market and economic spreads, the volume is turned up on fear—the fear of losing everything, including jobs and savings. When people in power—the kind of power provided liberally under a free market system—are faced with a crisis, they cry danger and claim that a "state of emergency" must be instituted. Finance steps in at the last moment to safeguard its own interests. It takes charge of governance and deploys its own techniques, claiming that it is different from regular people and knows what's good for them. The International Monetary Fund arrives to decrease national sovereignty. Soon it becomes obvious that this process, based on the same mechanisms that caused the crisis, is not mending the crisis but instead prolonging and aggravating it.

Whatever his faults, an elected figure ceases to matter, while an unelected one does, and indeed matters precisely because he is unelected. There is talk of taking away the people's right to vote, and replacing it with a system of drawing lots, so as to create a perfectly representative body, a true House of the People. The roots of democracy are yanked from the soil, and an ultimatum is handed down, with insistence that the public deficit problem can be cured with doses of democratic deficit. When these things happen, it is then difficult to stop or prevent social clashes. It's hard to get the toothpaste back in the tube, as the saying goes. When the decaying of spreads shakes our faith in ourselves and in the spirit of the European Union, then the risk is clear and the signs of a new fascism are beginning to emerge from a civilized Europe: *financial fascism, white-collar fascism.*

It is still very likely that even today, post-2007, we're heading for another 1933. After 1933, things went well in the United States. This was not the case in Germany, where the crisis was handled poorly. Yet today Europe still looks to Hoover and his disciples and heirs, rather than to Roosevelt. The former was the president of fear. The latter was the president of hope. Again, as we did in the era of the New Deal, we are confronting our destiny. As has been said, the people always do the right thing in the end, after having first made every possible mistake!

It would be the ultimate mistake to submit to this crisis, hoping to overcome it this way. To do this, or rather, to do nothing, to play the same video game forever will only call forth more dangerous monsters. Waiting for the stabilization of the financial market or a mythical recovery, waiting for inflation or even a war to save us would be the ultimate mistake, and a fatal one, because, again, we would just be paving the way for the next monster. All we would be doing is creating the next crisis, a worse crisis. The final crisis.

There is a workable exit strategy. It can be found in our recent past. We must and we can gather the courage to shape it, to understand it, to implement it. The courage to step off the wrong path, the path that more or less everyone—countries, governments, peoples—is still following. They are still victims of the primary myth of the twenty-first century, victims of their own belief in a system. That belief has been sharply challenged by the absolutism of the financial markets.

While the fear index continues to rise, we still have time. Hope can still prevail, as it prevailed over the Great Depression in 1933. We still have time to take control, to reorganize what we now call the market or the financial market, but what is in reality no longer an economic system but a chaotic jumble.

We can do this by anticipating and averting the current flood of events and phenomena rather than surrendering to them. We must reason before and not after events, acting on their causes and not their effects. We can begin by imposing a radical and fundamental separation between the *economy of production* and the *speculative economy*, preserving the former and disempowering the market-as-casino, either by forcing it to come to a rest, as on the biblical Sabbath, or arranging orderly bankruptcy proceedings, so that the people who gamble and lose are forced to pay for their losses and the rest of us are not.[4] We must put currencies back in the hands of the state, in the name and on behalf of the people. That will stabilize and balance public budgets. We must restore the authority of law and kick-start plans for public investment. Above all, we must value humanity, reason and spirit over self-interest. We must replace stones with bread; we must replace wolves with men. But before acting, we need to understand what has happened and what is happening and we must—and we can—do this before the financial market cashes out its Mephistophelian bank note. This is the aim and the purpose of this book. Not everyone will agree with this book, most likely. It will probably be refuted and rejected by the financial, political and academic powers that be, because today those powers believe that they—unchallenged—embody established power. And that's another reason you should read this book.

Any royalties from this book will be donated to charity.

[4] If you object to its characterization as a casino because you find it over the top, I'd refer you to this quotation: "When the capital development of a country becomes a by-product of the activities of a casino, the job is likely to be ill-done" (J.M. Keynes, *The General Theory of Employment, Interest and Money*, 1936).

I
Three Tragic Mistakes

It is said that people learn about geography in times of war and about the economy in times of crisis. It is said that the truth is never clearer than in the middle of the darkest night. Those things are true.

Five years into the crisis, it is now clear that in the West, politicians on the right as well as the left have made three mistakes. Three tragic mistakes, all connected to each other: They couldn't tell the difference between a normal economic cycle and a historic crisis; they used public money to foot the bill for private gambling; and they confused fake rules with real ones. In short, they have passively accepted finance's victory over politics. The latter remained hidden inside the Trojan horse of the board that was put into place in 2008 with lots of noise about how it would secure worldwide "financial stability."

Why were these errors made? Why was the first historic opportunity to implement an exit strategy not taken? Mainly due to a perverse combination of logical flaws of vision and power and overstepping of bounds.

The first flaw, which involved both vision and power,

is rooted in Western politics. The last time Western powers made an important political decision was twenty years ago, when they launched globalization. That decision has had a violent, distorting and forceful impact on the natural rhythm and progression of history. A determined and educated elite sought to achieve globalization in order to condense and accelerate history. Now, twenty years after this important decision and as a direct result of it, the political sphere is basically a vacuum. It's as if making this important, historical and controversial decision left the political world gasping for breath. Why did this happen? Picture this: Countries take a sharp intake of breath and suck in all the unique elements of national character. Globalization takes hold, and those countries exhale forcefully and spew those characteristics all over the world—a world now dominated by the global market. How did things get this way?

For centuries, political power has been concentrated in the hands of nation-states. But the nation-state is a mechanism constructed to function in a closed territorial domain. State-controlled territory formed a natural container for agricultural, mineral and, later, industrial wealth. The nation-state controlled the wealth and was invested in what was once known as *forum*, meaning the power to wield political monopoly: minting coins, collecting taxes, meting out justice. In breaking the historical chain between state, territory and wealth, in opening up cracks and spaces and weakening the power of boundaries and borders, globalization has eroded the old mechanisms of control and discipline. As a result, the power of the state is at an all-time low. Meanwhile, with the old boundaries knocked down, financial wealth, the most strategic and increasingly important type of wealth, has grown even stronger. Winged, stateless and irresponsible, it flies across and over territories, outside the birdcage of the nation-state, in the new skies of the international republic of money.

A dual world has been created. Governments still exist, of course, but they've been weakened by the territorial dominions' loss of political power. They inhabit the lower level of this new world, where they are increasingly unimportant and useless. They are dinosaurs living in unprotected reserves, slowly heading toward extinction. Meanwhile, the market and finance are firmly established on the upper level. From there, they are becoming increasingly powerful and transcendent. Up there in the heights, they are able to absorb a great deal of power. A new, never before seen political mechanism allows them to suck up more and more power. This mechanism is built on a global scale. It is replacing our traditional social dynamics, such as Machiavelli's "tumult," Spinoza's "multitude" and Marx's "class war." It may be more banal than those dramatic, romantic, heroic movements, but it has equivalent or greater revolutionary impact.

"Classic" politics, established in the world of the nation-state, languishing on the lower level, has begun to fray and slowly, gradually to dissolve. Its star is fading, by which I mean traditional ideologies and categories as well as specific political archetypes and individuals are no longer important. Perhaps that's why, in supply and demand terms, politics always offers more followers than leaders.[5]

A series of increasingly irrelevant and inconsistent politicians are now taking turns making the scene in this new globalized environment. With a few remarkable exceptions evenly divided between left and right, they have increasingly gray and flaccid ideas and policies. This cannot be offset with new ideologies, though

[5] This was not the case once, when the old political leaders, hardened by social conflict, conflicting ideologies, human adventure and even prison and war, were asked to make decisions for better or worse on the fate, future and destiny of their peoples. It is of course true that since the early 1900s, politics has been much more about economics. But that economics was a hard economics, one of iron and labor, of salaries and class conflict. An economics that did not modify but rather upheld the original structural characteristics of politics. In any case, this transfer of power from politics to economics did not last long. With World War II and above all with the Cold War, politics in fact returned to politics, to the great politics of war and peace. It is only now that politics seems to have essentially become economics, but a very specific type of economics: financial economics. There is therefore a great difference between the past and the present. The old summits were held between leaders, both Western and Communist, who knew what they were talking about and effectively and decisively chose the policies to pursue, and sometimes those not to pursue. There is a different kind of leader at today's summits. These are leaders who know very little of the über-technical topics they are required to address, or rather, which they claim to want to address (banking recapitalization, deleveraging, basis points, etc.) and who, above all, are unable to do very much and attempt in vain to chase after the financial market.

that doesn't stop people from trying. For example, a few years ago there was an attempt to create a movement around the "third way," a kind of centrism. Many of these new ideologies seem like parodies of the old and "glorious" ideologies.

As the power of traditional politics has decreased, the power of another sector is growing rapidly to fill the void: Finance is overtaking politics. Finance is powerful because of its ability to mobilize and concentrate colossal interests. It's powerful due to its successful ideology, powerful because of its ability to create credit for itself in the media for the market in general and for the financial market in particular, positioning both of them as new superefficient entities that can take the place of the old politics. A large cast of characters with a blend of ingenuity and political cunning has appeared on the scene (along with, of course, some honest but modest types). These include neophytes, ventriloquists and lobbyists, repeating verbatim the market liturgy of financial orthodoxy. Politicians and financiers, financiers and politicians are thus fused together by faith and fetishistic thought: They all wear the same uniform.

All of this has gone unnoticed. It has been tolerated and experienced passively. For years, no one made any trouble. As long as things were going well and linear progress continued to be made, the triumphal march of the global market lasted. Only when the crisis hit and we got into difficulty did the void in contemporary politics become clear in the West. Indeed, it continues to become clear. In the wake of the crisis, there is an imbalance between the dramatic gravity of the phenomena that are occurring and the political inability to understand them, let alone confront them. Politics cannot seem to push itself to understand. It can't seem to overcome the tendency to lie. Politics can't tell the people the truth, and without doing so will never have the right spirit for the new times ahead. Both the words and actions of politics need to change. For evidence, just take a look at the official communiqués made public at the end of international summits, the *ipse dixit* reviews and reports. Why was our country and the entire Western world so blind?

It was because politics are in awe of finance, and they feel inferior to it. Western governments have been too easily persuaded to act as business committees for the financial world. They've done this in good faith or in bad faith and in different ways and with varying intensity, but they've done it.

Young people were the first to understand. Then not-so-young people, and now most people—long before politicians—have realized what's happening. They're starting to look around. They're refusing to stick with programmed thought. They are beginning to protest and to denounce both politics and finance. Before we discuss that any further, we should take a look at how the mad and deceptive system of active and passive material structures and cultural substructures and obvious and secret interests have led the Western political world to make three tragic mistakes over the last five years.

Mistake Number One: Mistaking a Historic Crisis for a Normal Economic Cycle

On the morning of the July 15, 1789, Louis XVI awoke to the news that the Bastille had been stormed. He turned to the Duke de la Rochefoucauld-Liancourt and asked, "Is it a revolt?" The duke responded, "No, Sire, it's a revolution."

Perhaps later the king, too, began to use the word "revolution," but given his state of mind, he likely continued to attribute the meaning of the old word to this new word. That may be why he ended up at the guillotine—because he persisted in thinking that it was a revolt, rather than a revolution.

Western governments had the same reaction when they first got wind of the crisis in 2007.

Creators and victims of their own destiny, Western governments continued to think, or rather not to think, as they always had. They participated in a kind of collective illusion. This illusion was the idea that there could be a speedy recovery. It is true that at international summits, politicians began almost immediately to use the word *crisis*, a word from the ancient Greek that means a rupture in continuity, a discontinuity, a change in paradigm. However, due to mental inertia and for reasons of self-interest, politicians continued to think, to hope and to delude themselves that the crisis was only a phase in the economic cycle. They may have admitted that the cycle was more dramatic than usual, but still they saw it as only an economic cycle. Inability to distinguish between the ordinary and the extraordinary set in. This inability to understand new words and form new modes of thought was encouraged both by the superficiality of the analysis and the power of the interests involved. We have deluded ourselves that we can manage the crisis without understanding where it came from and why it happened. The fact that the crisis arose from a revolutionary combination of new geography, new technology and new ideology has never been acknowledged.

Nor has it been acknowledged that the crisis arose from globalization. Yet when the great divide between liberal West and communist East collapsed, globalization suddenly united the world under a new mercantile geography, stateless and irresponsible.

Computerization has gradually transformed a huge and strategic piece of the economy into electronic symbols and signs that can be circulated around the globe instantaneously, via the Internet. The Internet is the homeland of the new finance. Computers with their artificial intelligence can automatically multiply the number of trades and the number of parties involved, potentially to infinity. As a result, almost as if by magic, the volume of financial wealth expands.

Finally, *marketism* was at work. What is marketism? An ideology that subverted the old liberal political order and first theorized and then legitimized the market's universal domination of the state and then everything else.

As a result of globalization, the structure of the world

and the speed at which things move have changed drastically in just twenty years. This has never happened before in human history.[6]

And it is precisely globalization and the time and the way in which it was implemented that caused this crisis.

To think that such an intense and vast change in the order of things could happen without causing any damage was, and still is, deluded.

However, the cause and effect relationship between globalization and the crisis is still almost entirely absent from current economic and political analyses. Perhaps that's because globalization has done a great deal of good in many parts of the world, so it is widely considered to be inherently good.

Without seeing the full picture, Western leaders more or less all deluded themselves that they could coast along and bridge the crisis, moving from the past to the future as if nothing had happened.

They reacted as if past, present and future form a

[6] Of course, as far back as the 1800s, for example, at the time of the so-called gold standard, the market was already international. But the underlying political structures that were in place remained national, and were paradoxically so powerful that they were able to self-destruct, as was the case during the two world wars, which were perhaps just the same war with a long armistice in between. The same was more or less true of the period that followed, the Cold War period: There was an international market, certainly, but there were still true nation-states. The international extension of the market is one thing, but it's quite another thing for globalization to create the new phenomenon of a transnational marketist absolutism.

continuum and ignored the radical and abrupt discontinuity that is the hallmark of crisis.

After the first dramatic G20 in Washington (December 14 to 15, 2008), the imperative of survival took hold, and tension slowly faded. Thus, political thought and action universally turned toward an "exit strategy" based on a political palimpsest that was widely agreed upon. For the most part, that strategy aimed at returning as quickly as possible to precrisis economic levels. It had clearly been accepted that these levels could be reached again, minus several years of growth.

The prevailing stance was to act as if the crisis had been a mere incident on the positive and progressive road of automatic growth typical of the global market, rather than a dramatic turning point in history.

So, with a mentality and political approach ill-suited to the times, long-term problems have been dealt with using short-term methods, and extraordinary problems have been dealt with using ordinary methods. The major force at play is a form of inertia, inherited from the past.

Few understood that a vast proportion of the wealth created over the past twenty years was in fact based on debt, meaning it was based on nothing. It was wealth on paper that was responsible for the original crisis. From the stimulus applied to support demand for consumer goods, to money dropped from helicopters, to so-called quantitative easing, discretionary amounts of new money were issued electronically, intended to provide banks with all the cash they "needed." This is still going on, in a process analogous to trying to cure an alcoholic of his disease by providing him with booze. There still is no grasp of the fact that we have not been and are not facing a short-term liquidity crisis, caused by a lack of faith or circulating capital, but rather a structural solvency crisis caused by a twenty-year excess of debt. It was precisely the uncontrolled leverage of debt that first supported the instant miracle of globalization. Today, we've received the bill.

The bill for what? We speak, almost always now, mostly superficially, of the "subprime crisis." This is a reference to the loans that were granted freely and haphazardly to almost anyone who applied for one. These are "subprime" because they were granted not to reliable (i.e., "prime") clients, but to financially insecure clients. These loans were then wrapped up together in junk packaging and circulated on the financial market so that the associated credit risk could be foisted onto others. To believe that this is *the* phenomenon that caused the crisis is to confuse a part with the whole, the effect with the cause.

In reality, the subprime sector, while still very important, is only a part of the problem. It is just one technique that was used to create the artificial appearance of financial wealth, which in turn is used to sate the American demand for consumer goods manufactured in Asia and sold in America. This exchange mechanism is typical of globalization. This was no small thing. But subprimes were still only one aspect at the heart of a much more vast phenomenon: the new intercontinental and uncontrolled imbalances between enormous masses of work, goods and capital that are typical of globalization. These dramatic events culminated in an imbalance between massive amounts of credit and massive amounts of debt; between creditors and debtors; between private and public interests; between people, banks, societies and nation-states. This last type of imbalance is now widespread in Europe. In the end, it will result in an imbalance between continental blocks, between the United States and China. These imbalances could create new storms or even risk of a new war.

First there was the illusion. The illusion that a new type of capitalism would gradually emerge, titanic in its strength, cosmopolitan in its new financial philosophy, evangelical in its benevolent protection of the globe. Then, precisely because of the interconnected and colossal asymmetries that had been created, the crisis hit. And this crisis was badly handled, as if hardly anything had changed, and as if everything could go back to the way it had been before.

Mistake Number Two: Paying Off Private Gambling Debts with Public Money

In the Gospel, it is written that new wine must be poured into new bottles, for if new wine is poured into old bottles, "the new wine will burst the bottles and be spilled."

And this is exactly what happened. Five years ago, many of the major global banks had failed, and Western governments saved them by pouring rivers of public money into them. Generally speaking, five years ago the governments in the West had a strategic and absolute power over the failed and failing banks, the power of life or death. But the only way they used this power, absurdly enough, was against themselves. Five years ago, Western governments could do what they wanted. And as a result, many bankers at the World Economic Forum in Davos in 2008, for example, asked only to be nationalized! Instead, Western governments passively chose to do what the finance and banking system of power wanted: to buy time, to make a show of changing the rules, in the meantime damaging public finances with the losses accumulated over years of financial gambling. Then they could carry on as before, or even worse.

It was one thing to avoid an instantaneous collapse, and it's true that if circulation of liquidity had been completely blocked, it would have been like stopping blood from circulating within a body, and the heart, the financial system, would have stopped abruptly. However, even more serious action was taken later, and what was done was much worse.

The major failed banks were going to be "saved." The banks were considered "systemic." On the face of it, this can be justified: Banks are in effect essential to modern economic systems. They are vital parts of the whole and therefore systemic.

But it was in the application that this went terribly wrong. Precisely because they are systemic, banks should not have been permitted to operate like casinos. This opened them up to be attacked by viruses, or devastated by gambling plague.

Five years ago, the failed banks were supposed to be nationalized and/or radically reorganized. They were going to broken up into smaller entities, so that there were no more systemic banks considered too big to be allowed to fail. This could have happened. The banks could have separated their traditional business—storing savings and capital to finance companies, families and real investments—from speculative financial activity, which is quite different.

In short, separating productive economy and speculative economy could have saved the banks. Not by offering support for speculation and public guarantees, but on the contrary, by pushing speculation toward orderly bankruptcy proceedings. That way, speculators would have been saddled with the risks and costs created over the previous years of gambling.

Little or none of this has been done, however. Quite the opposite! Private debts have become public ones. Public capital has been supplied to failed banks almost unconditionally, with the objective or at least the final essential result of allowing the system to carry on as before: business as usual. The fact that some of the saved banks repaid public capital to governments does not contradict what is written above. In those cases, though public capital wasn't lost, the historical and political chance to take action against the causes of the crisis was lost. It makes no difference whether capital that has been disbursed is lost or returned: Whatever happened, the old system has been allowed to continue. Given the power and the political centrality of finance and the banks over people, we now think more about bank welfare than about social welfare. The bill is passed on to the community, which is left systematically exposed to the system's interconnected risks, as we are now seeing.

Mistake Number Three: Confusing Real Rules with Fake Ones

Not only should we have treated the banks differently, but when the crisis did explode, the strategic role of the rules could have and should have been understood. The market had become global, so the law could not remain local. The global market should not have been left without law and regulation, dominated by the enormous anarchic imbalances that would result—more of a chaos than a system. According to nature and reason, the law should and could have been aligned with the structure of the material reality underlying it: If one is global, the other must be global, too, as outlined in the 2009 Encyclical Letter *Caritas in veritate*. Five years ago, there could have been a move made toward creating a new set of market laws. We needed something new, in ancient terms, a new *tabula mundi*. A new global legal standard. We had an opportunity to rewrite the new rules of global capitalism, and we should have taken it.

This process of alignment between economy and law can be traced back to a proposal made by Italy at the 2009 G7. It asked for new global legal rules to be written and included in a new type of multilateral international treaty (more on this later). But this proposal was quickly blocked by the opposition. Artfully, the terms of the issue were muddled; the problems were confused with their outcome. The original crisis was essentially financial in nature, it was said, so there should be rules for finance, but not for the global economy as a whole. It was then suggested that these financial rules, which would have to be complex, should not be imposed by governments, but rather they should be written and proposed by the banks themselves, given their superior "technical skill" in this area. Study that phrase carefully and you'll note that the adjective cancels out the noun, which gives you an idea of how much common sense the whole thing embodies.

Thus, that great Trojan horse named the Financial Stability Board was established (more on this later, too). The name of this entity (financial stability!) today paradoxically, ironically and grotesquely is its complete opposite. It exists for a diametrically opposed reason. But creating the committee bought time, and the government got sidetracked. The results are the opposite of the stated objective at the time: Rather than governments dictating rules to regulate finance, the financial world is dictating its rules to the governments.

What Has Changed Since 2008?

The Final Report of the National Commission on the Causes of the Financial and Economic Crisis that hit the United States starting in 2008 was published in January 2011.[7] The report's conclusions about these facts and events basically state that "the financial crisis was avoidable; huge failures in financial regulation and supervision have had devastating effects on the stability of the national financial market; dramatic failures in the management of society, and in the systems set in place to control risk in many systemic financial institutions, were key factors in the crisis; a combination of excessive debt, risky investments or opacity put the financial system on a collision course with crisis; the government was poorly prepared for the crisis, and its incongruous response increased uncertainty and panic within the financial market; that there has been a systemic decline in reliability and ethics; that the spark of contagion came from real estate loans; that OTC derivatives contributed greatly to the crisis; that the rating agencies only speeded up the process of financial destruction."

[7] Financial Crisis Inquiry Commission, The Financial Crisis Inquiry Report, Official Government Edition, 2011.

The question that we need to ask ourselves is this: Has anything changed since then? Since 2008? If anything has changed, has it been a change for the better or for the worse?

According to some estimates, the value of the speculative bubble is at about 1.5 quadrillion dollars, a number more suited to astronomy than economics! The mass of derivatives, that twisted form of finance, began to increase exponentially because the risk was shifted onto the interest rates on state bonds. States that saved finance were being thanked by being devoured.[8] But this

[8] According to the Bank for International Settlements (BIS), the notional value of over-the-counter derivatives (i.e., the financial bubble created in unregulated markets), reached a new high of 707.569 trillion dollars in the middle of 2011, that is to say, 100 trillion more than at the end of 2010. In fact, on December 31, 2010, the mass of over-the-counter derivatives came to only (only!) 601.046 trillion. Since 2008, or since the beginning of the crisis, the bubble has not become smaller, but it has remained stable. However, in 2011, the growth of the bubble began again, allowing it to establish a new record high. In order to have a point of comparison, according to the provisional estimates of the International Monetary Fund, in 2010 global GDP came to 62.911 trillion dollars, and this means that the mass of derivatives is worth 11.2 times the planet's GDP. Almost all of the recent growth can be attributed to gambling on interest rates, given that the notional value of contracts on rates rose, in only six months, from 465.260 to 553.880 trillion dollars. The credit default swaps also improved: From December 2010 to June 2011, the notional value outstanding went from 29.898 to 32.409 trillion dollars. In both cases, it seems obvious that there is a correlation between the growth of these volumes and the cause of tension regarding European sovereign debt. The states saved finance without conditions, and in response finance is now attacking the state without pity.

didn't just happen in the United States. Indeed, targeted speculation on food and foodstuffs continues, with its deadly arithmetic, to cause despair amidst the despair that already exists in the world's poorest countries.

Speculation has remained standard practice at the systemic banks. There are fewer of these banks than there were before, but this is offset by their greater power. For example, in the United States these banks went through an intense process of "creative destruction," and the number of large banks fell from fifteen to nine, but through this process the remaining banks became even more systemic.

So-called shadow finance takes place away from the light of any normal jurisdiction, yet it still has a volume equal to about half of the volume of regular financial activity!

It bears repeating: Governments created the current state of finance by giving away their capital and in so doing they put people's futures at risk.

The final result remains to be seen, but today we already know, from Bloomberg, that in a single day, December 5, 2008, in a way that served to kick-start rather than to combat the crisis, the U.S. Federal Reserve gifted the banking system with 1.2 trillion dollars.

Public debt ceased to be the medicine and became the illness. The crisis worsened as private losses were transformed into public debt. Public debt then created a new form of savage competition between the states. In this frenzied environment, 1 million euros worth of public debt was issued every eight seconds. Countries were alienated from each other by the burden of their public debt, which automatically increased the power of the financial world over the political world even further.

That's why, according to the International Monetary Fund, by 2020, public debt in the G20 countries will have risen to an average level of 120%. Obviously, that will be very difficult to sustain. Right now, the future of generations to come is being ruined.

What is especially paradoxical is that, within this circuit, many of the financial operators are not speculators at all, but institutional investors. The majority of these are pension funds, which invest the savings entrusted to them by the people in the financial market. Acting within the financial system, the pension funds themselves try to guarantee the pension interests of their clients by earning money. However, they are acting against their clients' interests by sending public services, as well as state finances, into crisis. They are actually destroying the very services that retirees rely upon more than anyone, everything from welfare to sanitation.

Ratings agencies are private entities, yet they have continued to play a public role.

No truly new financial regulation has been enacted, except for a few perverse items. There continue to be new rules for industry and manufacturing, but no new rules governing finance!

This is why various types of speculative funds (hedge funds, money market funds, exchange trade funds and so on) still exist. They are the same or worse, and they wear a protective armor of derivative and deviant instruments.

This is why so-called noncooperative fiscal jurisdictions have remained just as they were before.

This is why bankers' bonuses have not fallen in the least, as common decency would have dictated. Instead, they have increased.

This is why the financial elite still holds the reins of power. Having skirted failure for now, this elite dispenses moral wisdom and lessons in bankruptcy to young people, nations and governments. It will not hesitate to seize power directly.

This is why, from the standpoint of the real economy, the risk of a global recession has increased since the crisis began. That in turn would trigger another financial crisis. And so crisis follows crisis, and they continue to get bigger and more intense, leading to what the governor of the Bank of England commented had the potential to be the worst financial crisis ever.

This is the main reason why the crisis has not been defeated, even after five years of anticrisis policy. These policies have instead aggravated the situation, wasting time and resources in the form of trillions of dollars in capital and guarantees that have been spent or pledged.

It's hard to call this a "market" at all, at least in the conventional and historical sense of the word.

It's harder still to believe that behind all of this there is still a system, an economic system. On the contrary, behind all of this is a magma-esque combination of elements, forces and interests, each with its own specific dynamic, not coordinated within a system.

A system can be said to exist when it is possible in the present day to make rational predictions about its future. The solar system is a good example of a perfect system. The Soviet economic system was inefficient, but it was nonetheless a system. What we have today, created by the financial harm caused by marketism, fuelled by uncoordinated centripetal and centrifugal forces, is not a system, but instead chaos. And what's so irresponsible and crazy is that the various nation-states don't understand it and don't fight it. Instead they obey it and, what is more tragic, strive to obey it.

Today, the crisis wields impact not just on the economy, but on international politics, where it is responsible for damage that ranges from the structural and constitutional deformation of the European Union to the divergent and increasingly conflicting views of the world held by its two geopolitical powers, the United States and China.

Based on this, we can now begin to understand why we urgently need a different vision of the world and of Europe.

Our analysis will begin at the beginning, with globalization.

We'll then take a close-up look at both the mistakes that have been made and possible alternatives and solutions.

II
Dominant Capital

Looking back we can see that history over the last few years can be divided into two phases, or better, into two eras: before globalization and after globalization. These phases or eras differ from one another, despite their chronological proximity.

Before globalization, in the period stretching from the end of World War II until a few years ago, the world was divided neatly into two blocks: the Western, democratic block and the Eastern, communist block. A third part of the world fell outside of these two divisions and was aptly named the Third World. This area was hard to define politically and hardly relevant economically, even though it contained the largest proportion of the world's population.

The Western world had its own political and economic configuration. It was structured first under the Atlantic Charter (1941) and then later under the Bretton Woods Agreements (1944).

Only in the mid-1970s, under pressure from the communist ideological power spreading through the Third

World, from Asia to Africa to Latin America, did the West organize itself into a new political body: first, the G6 at the castle of Rambouillet in 1975, then, in Puerto Rico in 1976, the G7. This group was eventually consolidated under the so-called Washington Consensus (1981).

From its very beginnings in the 1980s, the G7 was a political body that represented more or less one-sixth of the world's population of 4 billion, or a little more than 600 million people. However, it controlled about 60% of the world's GDP. The G7 was unified by three codes: a linguistic code (English), a monetary code (the dollar) and a political code (Western democracy).

Externally it was threatened by communism, but it had the internal advantage of postcolonial revenue, for even after the colonies no longer existed politically, the West still collected money from them. This was not a just world, but it was a simple one. The traumas and complexities of the political world were external, irregular and sometimes violent geopolitical tensions and did not enter the area protected by the G7 scheme.

In the preglobalization world, the economy was above all about the market and the market was above all concerned with the exchange of material goods: industrial and agricultural products, containers of goods, barrels of oil, bushels of grain. Financial deeds and instruments were also exchanged, but these were structured in a very linear and elementary way. All of this was integrated and together represented the classic idea of the market as a place where goods are exchanged.

For every commercial operation, whether it involved an industrial product, a container of goods, a barrel of petrol, a bushel of grain or a bond, the number of financial transactions required was kept to a minimum of three or four. These included payment of the price, for example, or insuring the product against the risk of a change in interest or exchange rates. This was normal, given the usual gap between the date of the contract and the date of payment. It was in any case a small, instrumental, minimal set of transactions: The financial economy was still in the service of the real economy and not an independent variation of it, as it is now. According to Marx's definition, it was more or less "circulating capital."

Of course there was finance and of course there were banks. But they were mostly commercial or industrial banks that were also involved in the real economy, because they held household savings and capital and invested them predominantly in the real economy, at their own risk and while aware of their responsibilities.

In this simpler world, the most technological, useful and sophisticated financial innovation for decades was, and I'm not kidding here, the ATM machine. In this world, the nation-states were on top, conserving and exercising their historical political sovereignty, while finance remained below, in the service of the real economy, and thus an accessory, an instrumental entity.

It was a world that can be summed up in the diagram on the next page:

G7

Canada, France, Germany, Italy, Japan, United Kingdom, United States
About 60% of global GDP
Only about 600 million people
Out of 4 billion people worldwide

Then came globalization and the aforementioned great and historic divide between *before* and *after*. The timer went off on the old world of the G7 when the World Trade Center collapsed, and then it went off again when the financial crisis exploded.

Thus, after two centuries, the center-periphery relationship was definitively and suddenly brought to an end. I say suddenly, because in history, a period of twenty years is really very short.

At this point the omnipotence of one part of the world over the other parts, of the G7 over the rest of the world, was over.

The newest and most dynamic forces in the world had been incubating. They'd been developing for a while. These were economic forces with the highest growth rates of GDP in the world, as well as demographic forces, as the youngest part of the world's population shifted. These forces had been formed earlier and had been silently growing for decades outside of the G7.

Drawing strength from their new vitality, huge parts of the world suddenly freed themselves from the pull of the almost magnetic attraction that had, directly or indirectly, drawn them toward the "center of the world" for at least two centuries.

The vector of history ceased to be linear and instead became circular.

The world would no longer revolve around one place or two. This is why the world has come to be and will come to be so complex. It is an archipelago of continental masses, which causes huge economic, social and political imbalances.

The best thing about this change is that for the first time in history, changes to geopolitical relationships and the balance between states and holdings, between geographic and demographic areas, have been wrought exclusively by the economy rather than the usual sequence of economy-war-economy. So far no war! Even in these years of crisis, there have been no wars. At other times when such great imbalances were at play, war would have been a given.

However, I repeat, even without any wars, force and strength within the world has drastically shifted. We Westerners, Europeans in particular, suddenly find ourselves in unknown territory. We have passed from an age of certainty to one of uncertainty. In the West, in Europe especially, the age of colonialism, which was over years ago politically speaking, is now truly over. This age, which lasted up until only a short time ago, was an age in which the West, Europe, still at the center of the world, could plant its products and stock throughout the world, when it wanted, in the quantities that it chose, at the prices that it named. Things don't work that way anymore.

Overtaken by globalization, the old G7 was incapable of foreseeing let alone avoiding the crisis. This is why it has been replaced by the G20.

Unlike the old G7, the new G20 is a political body representing a huge population base—about 4.5 billion people in 2010. Unlike the G7, which exerted a real level of control, the G20 represents, but does not control, about 80% of the world's GDP.

The G20 is very different politically from the G7, starting with the fact that it is no longer united by the three old codes that united the G7. There is no linguistic code, because languages other than English are spoken with pride.

There is no monetary code, because other currencies besides the dollar count, and these currencies compete with each other: the euro and the Chinese renminbi, for example.

There is no political code, because types of political systems other than ancient Western democracy are developing their own strength and power.[9]

[9] Further notes on what happened in the world during the transition from the G7 to the G20 can be found in Appendix 4.

The new world of the G20 looks like this:

G20

Argentina, Australia, Brazil, Canada, China, the European Union, France, Germany, India, Indonesia, Italy, Japan, Mexico, Russia, Saudi Arabia, South Africa, South Korea, Turkey, United Kingdom, United States

4.5 billion people out of a world population of about 7 billion

What is really striking in this new world is the imbalance of size, the inversion and disassociation created in the relationship between the real economy and the financial mass, as shown in the diagrams that follow.

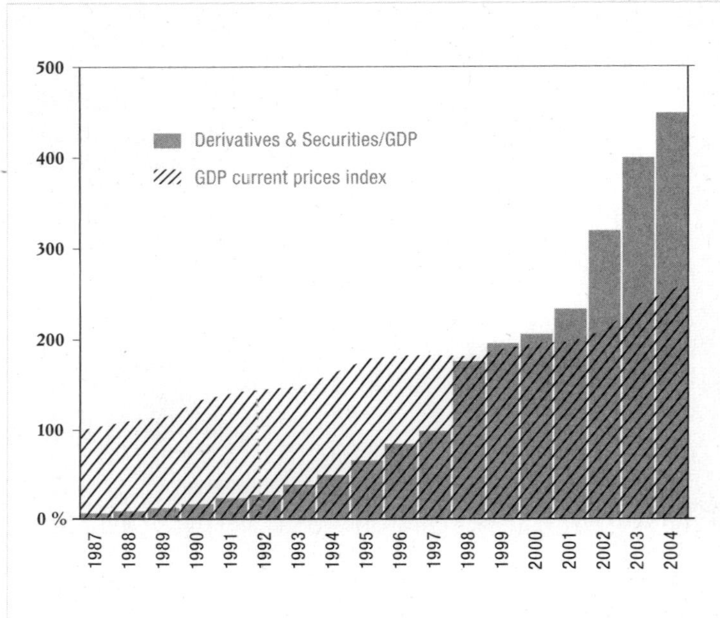

Fig. 1. The rise in derivatives in relation to GDP in the G10 countries (Belgium, Canada, France, Germany, Italy, Japan, the Netherlands, Sweden, the United Kingdom, the United States) and Switzerland.

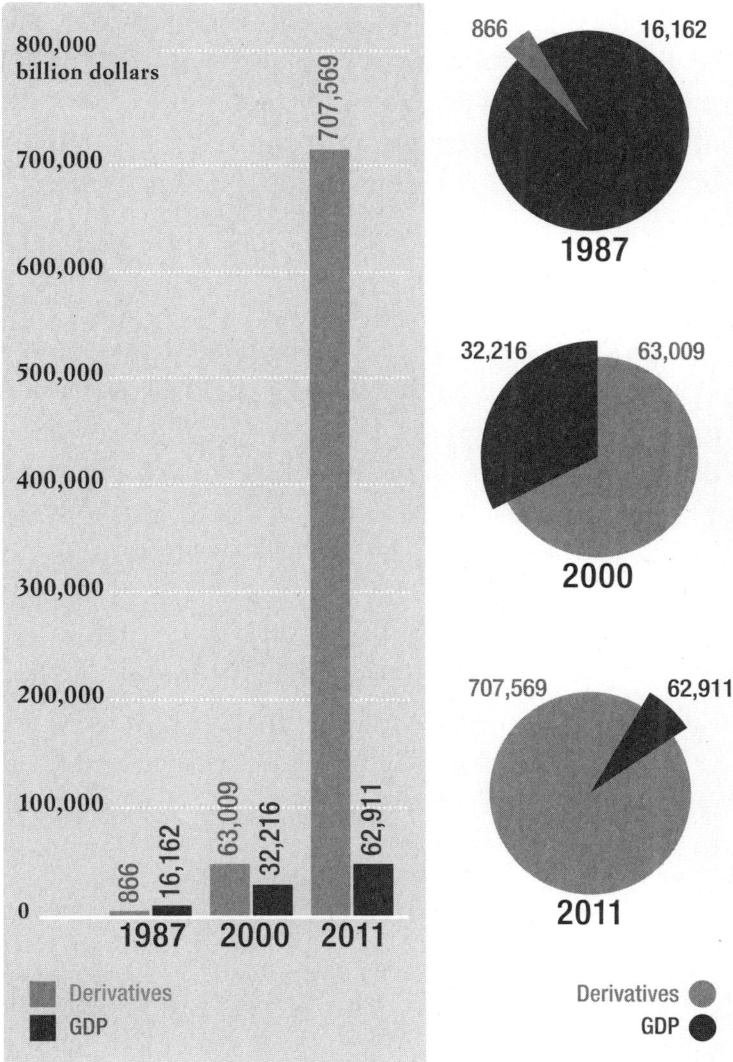

Source: ISDA, data given in billions of dollar. The data for 2011, as of June 30th, is from BIS

Fig. 2. Derivatives and world GDP, in two different diagrams that highlight the exponential growth of the financial economy after the start of globalization.

In the first diagram (Fig. 1), the shaded area represents Gross Domestic Product (GDP). The grey columns represent the volume of financial mass, made up of derivatives. The trends show not only that there has been truly monstrous growth in the financial mass, but that this has occurred and then developed on the back of globalization.

The agreement to free up world commerce, the World Trade Organization agreement, was signed in Marrakech in 1994 and set off globalization. Asia formally became a party to the agreement in 2001. As you can see, the economic dynamics in the diagram reflect these dates. The financial mass equals that of the real economy in the three-year period from 1999 to 2001 and then begins to grow unchecked.

To sum up the diagrams, the huge and aberrant financial mass is the fastest growing and most strategically expanding part of the world's economy. And it's growing exponentially as globalization and information technology develop and form a state of "dual independence."

The Independence of Finance from the Real Economy

The first form of independence is the independence of finance from the real economy. New financial operations are developed online, a liquid, silent and meta-real place. They are no longer accessories and instruments related to the real economy. They therefore can and do become autonomous ends in themselves.

As mentioned above, all of this has little or nothing to do with Marx's antiquated theory of "circulating capital": That liquid capital served as a lubricant that helped solids circulate. From the original seed of circulating capital sprang a new form of capital: what we now call "dominant capital." This new form of capital has, in only twenty years, developed autonomously through sequences of numbers and abstract signs, independent of the underlying tangible reality, independent of trade, and so able to multiply itself almost to infinity. It is so powerful that it is able to dominate all else: means of production, the workforce, states and our lives.

History and technological progress once occurred at a slow pace. They have now progressively accelerated, which first made possible and then produced this abstraction-substitution effect: the passage from the material of the things being traded to the metal of the money used in trading, followed by the passage from the paper of banknotes to the plastic of credit cards and eventually the passage from plastic to computer signs and symbols, which have limitless value.

The word capital comes from *caput*, ancient Latin for a head of cattle. In this new world, capital rarely refers back to underlying tangible goods at its source.

The Independence of Finance from the State

The second form of independence is the independence of finance from the state. It is independent because this new financial mass is made up of a type of money that is not minted by the state as money once was. The state is no longer sovereign in this sense. Instead, the money is minted by finance itself, for its own use and consumption. It's a type of money created in a unique way: first by creating debt and then by putting others into debt.

This is how states lost their sovereignty and finance created its own. This is how we've ended up with principles without money and money without principles. But all of this has not merely been an exchange of sovereignty, an arbitrage of power between states and markets. It was, and still is, a vertical climb up the global scale of risk.

In 2008, the uncontrolled explosion that took place in the financial mass created huge fallout in the underlying real economy, making it crash suddenly, as if it had dropped into an air pocket. This began with the destabilization of world commerce, the heart of globalization, as is evident from the diagram on the next page:

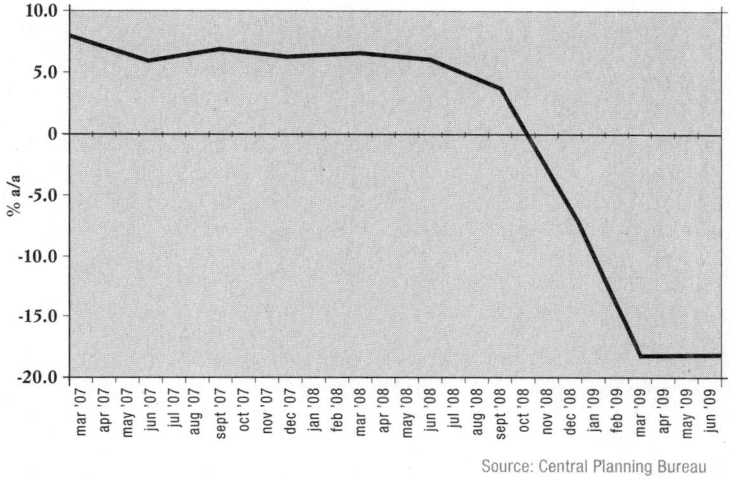

Fig. 3. The collapse of world commerce due to the financial crisis of 2008.

The problem today is that the crisis did not end in 2008. The risk that this same phenomenon will repeat itself, on an even larger scale, has not decreased. On the contrary, it has risen. The risk of a further destructive explosion, of an atomic meltdown, lingers and is even increasing. Over the last few years, the effects of the crisis have seen this mass expand enormously, even as states took on massive debt in order to "manage" it. Even public debt is a part of finance—not a minor part, and certainly not the least dangerous part.

Why is this so? Why was nothing done to avoid it? To understand, we must attempt to penetrate the mass of finance and examine up close its powerful yet risky mechanisms.

III
The Financial Market: When Geography Meets Alchemy

To get an idea of how the financial market functions today and how it continued to function even after the first explosion of the crisis, and to get a feel for its size and position, take a look at the "metamaps" below:

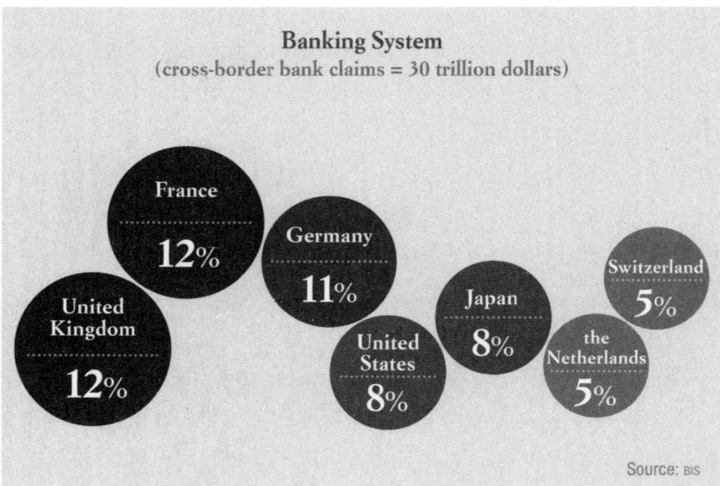

Fig. 4. Financial interconnections

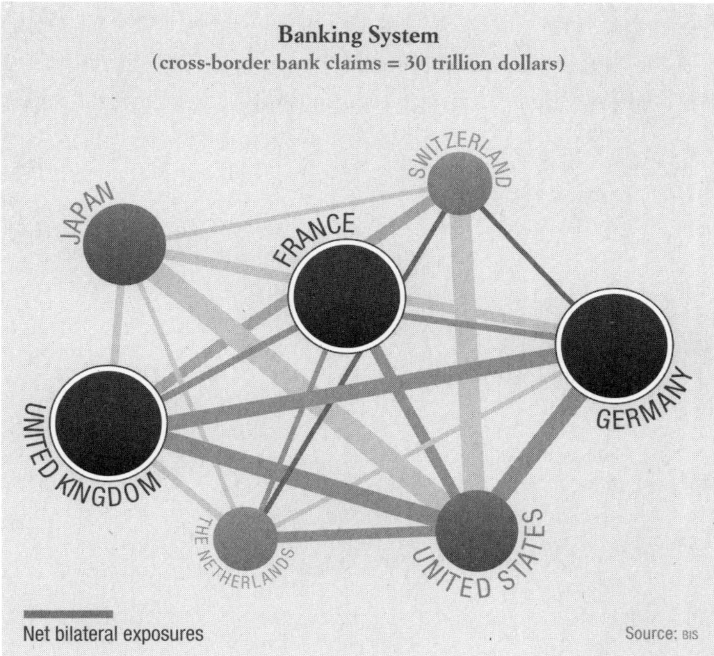

Fig. 5. The links between the main banking systems. The thickness of the lines is proportional to the volume of bilateral exposure.

A metamap is a special type of map that does not reflect conventional real-world geography, but instead uses other parameters, so that the items on the map reflect economic, demographic or financial realities. These are financial metamaps.

To make sense of the maps, in particular the meta relationship between finance and geography, consider that at a certain point on the financial metamap of the world, Iceland was much bigger than its physical geography, because it had become a giant hedge fund; the same goes for Ireland, which offered itself as a sort of "landing pad" for banking and financial mega-operations planned and managed outside of it.

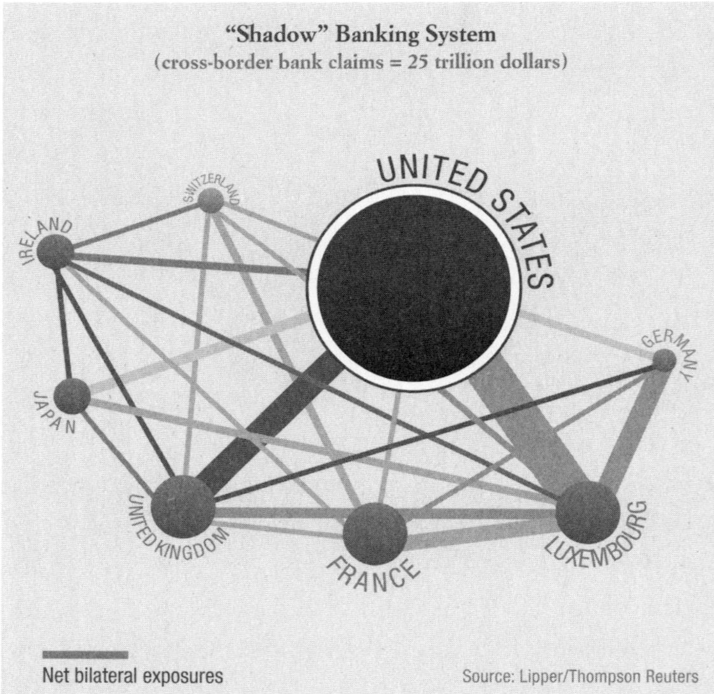

Fig. 6. The shadow banking system (money market funds, mutual funds, hedge funds, pension funds, exchange-traded funds).

But what matters today when trying to understand the makeup of the financial market is the relationship between finance and the law. This relationship was at one time relatively restrictive, but it is now absolutely open, modifying the geography, morphology and ultimately the very nature of capitalism itself. It wasn't always like this. Over the course of the centuries, in almost all geographical areas, and as a result of dramatic experiences, such as natural disasters, huge frauds, boom periods, financial marvels and speculative bubbles (various stages of mania and euphoria that all ended in panic, collapse, trauma and tragedies, and not just in a financial sense), the financial market gradually became more and more regulated. Over the last few years, however, an idea grew in opposition to this historical tendency toward regulation. In contradiction to the way things had worked for centuries, the idea began to circulate that it would be good for financial markets to achieve a kind of anarchic, untouchable independence.

Paradoxically, while the number of rules imposed on industry and manufacturing increased, the number of those to be imposed on finance decreased, in order to grant finance a privileged state of grace. It is important to note that the idea of financial deregulation emerged on the back of globalization and is—as in part sketched out above—linked to it in several ways, and those ways are interconnected with each other. There is the connection that moves upstream, through the ideology of deregulation, and the connection that moves downstream, through the imbalance between the global market and local law. This type of imbalance is typical of globalization. Finally, there is new information technology. Let's examine these causes in greater detail:

The Ideology of Deregulation

In political terms, the ideology of deregulation can be seen as a positive step toward getting rid of excessive regulation. It marks an attempt to combat the worst thing about modern society, today's orgy of legislation. However, for historic reasons of prudence provided above, deregulation cannot automatically be extended to the financial sector.

In fact in the United States, the center of the financial industry, the opposite occurred. Here, the process was carried out through two fundamental pieces of legislation: first the Gramm-Leach-Bliley Act (1999), which abrogated the earlier Glass-Steagall law (1933) that prohibited ordinary banks, commercial banks and insurance companies from commingling. Thus, banks were now allowed to mix credit, insurance and commerce, weakening the restrictions on debt leverage, reducing guarantee reserves and so on. Following on the heels of that was the over-the-counter (OTC) law in 2000, which legalized derivatives.

Then even more laws were eliminated. For example—one of many examples—the volatility trading stops law, which may have been naïve and ineffective, but was also appropriate, was eliminated. During a bear raid on a stock, this law would be triggered to stop it from spiraling until the same stock manifested not only sales but acquisitions. A market built on acquisitions as well as on sales would be restored. In other words, the law encouraged a market built on supply and demand, and not just on speculation.

Decisions to eliminate these laws were subject to intense political debate. Those decisions were based on the idea that the market is always right. More precisely, they were based on the idea that the king of all markets, the financial market, is always right. This political and legislative process did not end in the United States but spread from there, actively or passively, across the West.

The Imbalance Between the Global Market and Local Law

Imbalance between global market and local law was not ideological but geographical. Deregulation, after all, was based on the concept of a regulatory power. This imbalance opened the door for financial operators to break down standards and make way for activities that were not only unregulated, but antiregulated. That provided impunity: If it's not against any law, how can it be a crime? Still worse, it paved the way for activities positioned within fake jurisdictions in pseudostates that were internationally, unthinkingly and hypocritically recognized as real. The only rule was that there should be no rules except for fake ones. This is where shadow banking began to take shape. This type of banking works in the dark alongside official finance and indeed is often created by official finance.

New Information Technology

Finally, hand in hand with new reductionist legal strategies and with the opening of new geographic areas, new, instantaneous and global information technology has played a decisive role. Finance has access to computers, search engines, engineering and artificial technology.

Liberated from practically every legal restriction and thrown onto the world market, the mass of new finance became global, because in the Internet it found its ideal technical platform for expression and expansion. It found a homeland.

The Internet, where new wealth circulates and feeds itself uncontrollably, is growing exponentially in volume. It is self-replicating, an obvious result of techno-financial innovation. While the old capitalism was limited by the finite numbers of physical reality, the numbers of the new capitalism have no limits; they are potentially infinite precisely because they are meta-real or surreal. Thus, an interconnected and illusory capitalism has been born. Even now, postcrisis, this is a capitalism of abstract symbols: CDS, CDO, ABS and so on.

In this artificial and labyrinthine capitalism, you can sell something that you neither own nor have borrowed: true stocks, naked stocks, invented stocks.

In this capitalism, the false becomes true, the unreal makes itself real and people would rather believe in something that doesn't exist than something real, provided that the nonexistent thing is expressed through one of the mysterious mathematical formulas typical of techno-finance.

To get a feel for this, all you need to do is examine the following formula, which is actually one of the simplest (if you can believe it) formulas used to determine the actual value (if such a thing exists) of a credit default swap:

$$\begin{aligned} PV = {} & (1 - p_1)N(1 - R)\delta_1 \\ & + p_1(1 - p_2)\left[N(1 - R)\delta_2 - \frac{Nc}{4}\delta_1\right] \\ & + p_1 p_2(1 - p_3)\left[N(1 - R)\delta_3 - \frac{Nc}{4}(\delta_1 + \delta_2)\right] \\ & + p_1 p_2 p_3(1 - p_4)\left[N(1 - R)\delta_4 - \frac{Nc}{4}(\delta_1 + \delta_2 + \delta_3)\right] \\ & - p_1 p_2 p_3 p_4(\delta_1 + \delta_2 + \delta_3 + \delta_4)\frac{Nc}{4} \end{aligned}$$

At first glance, this formula looks like magic, and that's an apt description of the new finance. The ritualistic religion of the new capitalism feels like alchemy. In a bargain worthy of Faust and Mephistopheles, techno-finance creates wealth with a limited base in physical reality. Physical reality is too small for the greedy inhabitants of the world of techno-finance. Their desire for profit keeps expanding and is being pushed ambitiously toward infinity. Just look at the software designed for high frequency trading. With no human intervention, it sends thousands of trading orders out onto the open markets in just a few milliseconds. With all these orders, the effect on closing figures is usually minimal, but the consequent volatile extension of the "value" of the stocks is huge.

This is how the real and the surreal, the true and the false, get mixed up with each other. The nothingness becomes reality, and reality becomes nothingness. An upside-down world takes hold: what should reassure fails to do so, and instead multiplies the risk, spreading it, unlimited and out of control.

This is a capitalism in which a lot of people know very little and so try to give the impression of knowing everything. A world in which the one thing people know really well are the laws of the jungle of profit.

This is how the old order of the market deteriorated. From this chaos a new type of capitalism was born: financial capitalism, first dominant, and now, because of its nature, dying, a victim of its own chaos.

It is, of course, true that at the beginning of the crisis in 2008, faced with the chaos, we did again consider the question of the rules. However, as previously noted, the debate about the rules was restricted to finance alone and not extended to wider parts of the economy as it should have been. At the center of the debates were not governments but, at the request of the financial world, the Financial Stability Board, acting as the governments' proxy. This is why the crisis continues, as we will see in the next chapter.

IV
The Risk Is Ongoing

The same risk factors remain in place, and the explanation for their endurance lies primarily in the analysis of the activity, or rather inactivity, of the Financial Stability Board; but also in the workings of credit default swaps; in the criteria of Basel III; and, lastly, in the efficiency of the ratings agencies.

These cofactors work together, with a sum of negative effects greater than their parts, as we shall see below.

Financial Stability Board

In 2008, after the first shocks of the financial crisis, the Queen of England was visiting the London School of Economics. At some point, Her Highness turned to the teaching staff and asked, "Why did nobody notice it?" The same question could be asked today of the Financial Stability Board.

Yet there is a difference here, a difference in timing and responsibility: While the professors at the London

School of Economics were wrong in not predicting the crisis, the Financial Stability Board came into play after the crisis and so should have institutionally contributed by handling it, or at least by helping to determine ways to stop it; essentially, as its name suggests, it should have worked toward future financial stability. Yet in the four years since it was formed, the Financial Stability Board has done quite the opposite. What happened? What happened is that the Financial Stability Board operated as a sort of Trojan horse, built by finance to infiltrate politics and beat it at its own game. What happened is that the Financial Stability Board's mission has been and is insufficient in an astute and paradoxical world: It is excessively inefficient, an excessiveness represented by 16,000 pages, 80 kilometers of words.

Basically, the Financial Stability Board's mission was to reform finance to make it better and more just. Those who came up with this idea can look at the facts in order to evaluate whether it's been successful. The facts are these: The financial crisis continues and is worse than ever. Sometimes it takes the form of a "balance of imbalances." After serving a brief penance, the noncooperative jurisdictions have more or less the same amount of influence as they did before; the search for capital adequacy without debt limits is pretty much insane, and in any case perversely favors the systemic nature of the banks. The markets and ratings agencies once again render a verdict with no chance for appeal. Bankers' bonuses have reached record highs. In short: Has the

Financial Stability Board created, to paraphrase Candide, the most stable of all possible worlds?

How was the Financial Stability Board able to pull off this "reform" of the international financial system, controlling and monitoring both the process and the results? Through the unending growth of its activities.

It goes to extremes and beyond. For example, it set out to identify best practices by selecting them—strange but true—from those already employed by hedge funds! Not exactly a good example.

This compendium of conquests, more cleverly designed than the one that Leporello blurts out in *Don Giovanni*, is the Financial Stability Board's agenda and structure. It has increased and expanded beyond measure. Innumerable areas and subgroups have been created to address matters of secondary importance. Because of this overextension of its sphere of activity, and a commitment to seeing all sides, few conclusions can be drawn about what it does. Its overextension even serves to justify its delay in addressing more relevant topics. The only concrete regulatory and prudential measures that have resulted, such as the agreements on Basel III, were in fact previously developed in other forums (Basel Committee on Banking Supervision) and then presented as great successes of the Financial Stability Board. Not to mention, or rather purposefully mentioning, the fact that Basel III itself is a "capital sin."

To sum up, the Financial Stability Board approached its work from the wrong perspective from the get-go.

Since it came at the work from a technical and not a political perspective, it was never going to serve as a source of authority and rules.

Was the Financial Stability Board assigned a mission impossible? Yes. But we knew that from the start, when criticisms were framed as merely personal polemics. One could feel it as the years slowly passed. Why didn't the Financial Stability Board just stop what it was doing at a certain point and honestly admit it was powerless? What was and could have and should have been the true mission of the Financial Stability Board? In reality, the Financial Stability Board worked because it did not work. It was never intended to function. The real measure of its effectiveness is not that it turned around a crisis or stopped one from occurring in the future. It is meant to be judged not by the rules that have been created, but by the rules that were not created. Or worse, by the rules that were created poorly, so that the technical failures that caused the crisis to begin with are now codified. Because the Financial Stability Board's real function was merely to buy time for finance, allowing it first to survive and then to return to center stage, where it wields just as much if not more power than before. And that's not all.

Five years after the crisis exploded, it is obvious that the factors that caused the crisis not only persist, but are growing, starting with an excess of debt.[10]

[10] For further information on the Financial Stability Board see Appendix 5.

Credit Default Swaps

Credit default swaps are the prime example of today's financial madness. Originally, credit default swaps were genuine insurance instruments. No more. Today, credit default swaps are the most reckless insurance policies you can imagine. Let's look at how and why this is the case. A normal insurance contract is a bilateral contract between two parties, drawn up in order to insure one party (the insured) through the second party (the insurer), against a specific risk (faced by the insured), covered by the reserves of the other party (the insurer).

Credit default swaps don't work like that anymore. The risk is no longer a risk faced by the insured party, because with a credit default swap you can insure yourself against a risk faced by a third party. For example, if in the real world I can take out fire insurance to protect my house, in the world of credit default swaps I can insure myself against the risk that your house will burn down. Given that the cost of the policy is only a fraction of the worth of the asset that it insures, I will profit greatly if your house does burn down. But I can make money even simply by going around and saying that I smell smoke, or that a fire is about to break out. The credit default swap market disproportionately expands this type of opportunity.

So a layer of speculation has been added on top of the original insurance policy. Credit default swaps are products that are listed on a market, so it is possible to speculate on their value. That transforms an instrument that covers risk (hedging) into an instrument that creates and fuels instability in the system. Today, almost the entire world is covered in a network of credit default swaps whose subjects are the "houses" (meaning the stocks and bonds) of others, and that bear no specific or direct relation to the actual risk. In fact, with the traditional compact between two parties and one risk seeming no longer to apply, suddenly everything seems to be insurable, as if someone or something could insure someone else against the risk of the end of the world. Real money is put into false finance, so that everyone speculates, but in the end no one is really insuring.[11]

The Basel III Criteria

Basel is a peaceful Swiss city, situated on the banks of the Rhine. Its primary businesses and products, listed in ascending order of the danger they pose to society, are watches, pharmaceuticals, chemicals, insurance, banks—banks that were especially important in the time of the Third Reich—and, lastly, the international regulation of credit.

That last item was only recently added to the list. The first Basel agreement (Basel I) dates back only to 1988, and twenty years later it was superseded by Basel

[11] For further information on credit default swaps, see Appendix 6.

II. Unfortunately, this agreement was implemented in 2007 and 2008. It was immediately followed by the crisis, which led it to be tossed out. At first, it was presented as the new frontier of cautious vigilance. Unfortunately, in spite of the Basel Committee, this vigilance turned out not to be cautious at all.

Down but not out, the Basel Committee put in place a new package of international banking regulations called Basel III. In July 2011, the European Commission accepted the main recommendations of that agreement.

The major modifications introduced in Basel III address three aspects of the banking system: capital (starting in 2013); liquidity (starting in 2015); and leverage (starting in 2018).

As far as capital is concerned, a strengthening of the minimal financial requirements is planned, through an increase in the quantity and quality of capital.

Special liquidity coefficients will be introduced to avoid paralysis in the credit market. Financial leverage, which has relieved the huge debt bubble, is in fact one of the origins of the crisis and should be drastically reduced. Meanwhile, it is also the cause of huge profits from speculation and, consequently, bankers' bonuses.

It will come as no surprise, then, that the Basel Committee didn't make any real progress at all. That's why new standards won't be implemented until 2018. Here's the question: If I were about to drive off the road in my car, I could put my foot on the brake pedal and apply the brakes when necessary. Applying the brakes, in the world of global finance, would mean launching a process of deleveraging to reduce the exposure to risk and would consequently reduce profits and bankers' bonuses. So what is the underlying philosophy of Basel III? The response is to gun the engine. Instead of applying the brakes, why not boost the banks' capital?

Basel III basically takes off in one direction and then ends up going in a direction completely opposite from the one that any person with common sense would expect.[12]

The Ratings Agencies

Information about ratings agencies is rife with inaccuracy and hypocrisy. They are nominally private, and as such they are unregulated and cannot be disciplined according to specific rules. That is only partially true. This is a skewed version of the truth. It is true that ratings agencies, as private entities, are not formally, officially subject to discipline. But there are some highly important rules and regulations that affect them and consequently legitimize them. This is true of the European Central Bank for example; the same goes for the European Securities and Markets Authority and so on. Basel II and then Basel III called for the use of valuations performed by external parties (these very ratings

[12] For further information on Basel III, see Appendix 7.

agencies) and considered them essential and decisive in calculating the risk of the assets in banks' portfolios.

Because ratings agencies are recognized by official bodies but still remain unregulated, they are important. What's more concerning is that they themselves have the potential to cause systemic risk. Their opinions are still the cornerstone upon which global finance, a structure worth ten times the value of world GDP, rests.

The agencies' opinions create and destroy wealth, promote and condemn entire companies, banks and states. These ratings remain just "opinions," for better or worse. If ratings had a direct legal value, as auditing has a legal value, episodes such as the Lehman Brothers crash would have had more consequences for the ratings agencies. Arthur Andersen, a powerful auditing company, was virtually ruined after it was learned that it had certified Enron's false balance sheets. Ratings agencies on the other hand are private and therefore not officially regulated. They were never held accountable for the crucial role they played in the subprime fiasco, for example.

From the perspective of the market, the precycle influence of the publication of a rating is obvious, above all when the rating constitutes a downgrading, and if this occurs within a negative market situation like today's. Prices, interest rates and spreads shift immediately after such announcements, like crazy silver balls in a pinball machine, where the two flippers are ratings and credit default swaps.

On the institutional side: nothing. Since 2009, the European Parliament and Council have taken deliberate steps to create and impose a list of categories, transparency requirements, restrictions in case of a conflict of interest, and external control on the part of the European Securities and Markets Authority. But so far, they've done nothing else.[13]

[13] For further information on ratings agencies, see Appendix 8.

V
Greece and Europe

Chaos, annihilation, abyss, collapse, catastrophe, a threat to the world. These are examples of recent political language. Since autumn 2011, even official European rhetoric has been less conventional than normal. In Europe they speak of an "unexpected event," of an "acceleration of the unfolding of the crisis," of "severe stress," of a "warning within the European Union."

What happened? What happened, and what is still happening, is that the second monster in the video game popped up in Europe. This European monster is larger than the first one, larger than the American monster of 2008. Today Europe is at the epicenter of a crisis that is not only different from the American one, but also much more serious. More serious because it is not limited to private interests but instead has spread to public ones; it is not confined to the banks but affects the various states as well, thus suddenly melding the two forms of previously recognized crisis: a banking crisis and a state crisis.

This crisis has been made even worse by the fact that the combination of these two forms of crisis is manifesting itself in the European environment. On the one hand, that could encourage a chain reaction, as in an atomic meltdown, because Europe is connected by a common market and a common currency. On the other hand, Europe seems incapable of handling the crises with the vision and political strength required.

This is not just a crisis of individual banks or states, but rather it is a crisis of the whole economic and political architecture of Europe. Given that Europe is not only the richest part of the world, but also an area that is heavily connected to the rest of the world, it generates the risk of a world crisis. The so-called systemic banks were deemed too big to fail. States, too, are now labeled too big to fail, to which we might cynically respond that that may as yet not turn out to be true! At this point we can say the same of Europe: Europe is too big to fail. Or is it?

This isn't to say that the American crisis hadn't already reached Europe in 2008, or that parallel to the American one, a crisis similar to the American version did not manifest itself. However, that was only a sort of migration, a shift of that crisis from one side of the Atlantic to the other, or rather a local version of that same type of crisis. There was no mutation of the crisis into a larger, different form, no sign of a second monster.

This European monster appeared first in Greece.

In some parts of the world, more history is produced than can be consumed *in loco*, so the surplus history is exported. In past centuries, this was true of the Balkans.

Then it became true of Greece. Greece has produced and today exports a certain type of history: the history of bankruptcy. Not only its own bankruptcy, but that of Europe as a whole, which could, in a domino effect, spread around the whole world.

Greece itself represents only a small part of Europe—a part that is small in population, at least, with only about 11 million people, little more than the average European region—and in industrial production, comprising about 2% of Europe's GDP. Precisely because it is so small, the case of Greece could have and should have been dealt with relatively easily. As we have seen, the reality has been exactly the opposite. It is precisely this imbalance, between a small economic problem and its colossal political mismanagement, that has increasingly undermined and continues to undermine the foundations of confidence in the euro. "If you haven't been able to intervene here, what will you do when something happens in a larger region?" they mutter from the outside.

Greece's entry into Europe, mostly based upon its history as the homeland of Plato, was and is a problem due to the country's almost premodern political and administrative structure.

Modern democracy is based on a classic parliamentary principle: No taxation without representation. In Greece, that principle has been inverted and deformed. In that country, there is representation *without* taxation, which then produces an excess of combined public debt and tax evasion. Consequently, the relationship between public rights and public duties has been distorted immeasurably, and it is unacceptably uneven. The public administration is feeling the dramatic effects of this.

There is another problem with the way Greece joined Europe: It submitted a shadow public budget along with its official budget, which was itself rigged.

Yet another problem lies in the way the case of Greece was handled in and by Europe: two consecutive years of errors, first in the estimation of the extent and dynamics of the Greek crisis, second in the choice of tools employed to mend it. These could have and should have been only European tools, used with pride. Yet eventually Europe threw up its hands and accessed international funds, starting with aid from the International Monetary Fund.

Yet another problem was fuelled by the subsequent contradictory opinions and announcements. A tone-deaf choir, a cacophony: Greece will be saved. No, it won't. Greece will default. No, it won't. This was a choir with too many voices: governments, authorities, institutions, central and private banks.

Still another problem was the effect created in Greece by the restorative financial treatment applied there: Before the crisis, Greece's public debt was equal to 119% of its GDP; today, it is 150%, and it is predicted to soar to 190% soon, mostly due to the recession that followed the crisis. Just think what it means when steps are taken to help, and rather than public debt decreasing, the GDP falls!

This problem is spreading contagiously from Greece to the rest of Europe, causing catastrophe throughout the world.

Another issue is that the crisis in Greece has paralyzed and gummed up the European political machine; the more it needs to work and function to manage the crisis, the less it works and the less it functions. The Greece case exposed the fact that the European political machine used to work and function, but in an artificial way. For at least two decades, the game was being played in a lucky world, an environment that was unusual because of the substantial absence of any real problems.

And so we've arrived at the final fatal question: Can Greece leave the euro? Or not? No, they say, firstly for legal reasons. The exit of a country from the euro was not foreseen in the established euro treaty. Indeed, it was designed to make exit impossible: "All those, such as myself, who had the privilege of holding the pen to write the first version of the Maastricht Treaty had really committed ourselves to ensuring that an exit would not be possible. We carefully forgot to write the article that would allow a member-state to leave. That's not very democratic, but it was a great guarantee for making things more difficult, so that we would be forced to move forward together" (Jacques Attali). This recalls an enlightened saying of Goethe's: "In the first step we are free, but by the second we are slaves."

The answer is no, they say, for reasons both economic and symbolic: the classic risk of the *simul stabunt aut simul cadent* (united they stand and united they fall). The inherent risk begs a question: Who's next after Greece? And where will the domino effect lead? A double euro? The end of the euro? Underlying all those questions is a primary and essential question: What caused and continues to cause such a complex crisis within Europe?

If we compare the first and second monsters, meaning the American case and that of Europe, it's obvious that there is an essential political difference between the United States and Europe. In the United States, the crisis was from the start and still is now above all a banking crisis, resolved with strong and concentrated political action from the government. In the United States, a crisis remains only a banking crisis and doesn't turn into a state crisis. That will be true as long as the country retains its strong, almost imperial federal power, which guarantees burgeoning public debt based on its ability to mint unlimited quantities of money.

In Europe on the other hand, everything is very different. First of all, the structure of the crisis is very different: It's not just a banking crisis; it's also a public debt crisis. Finally, it is a different crisis above all because of the different and weaker political environment in which it has manifested itself.

The United States is a federal country, with a federal government and a federal currency and a true central bank. Because of this, it could and still can intervene in its banking crisis instantly and powerfully, in one day, with one action, with one political decision. The decision, for example, to release new quantities of both federal debt and federal currency. When the financial crisis erupted, the public hand suddenly became visible, and it immediately replaced the invisible hand of the market. All of this was possible because in the United States, not only is there a public hand, but there is only one public hand.

In Europe it's different. Yes, Europe is a single geographical continent, with a single market and a single currency, but it is not a federal state. It doesn't have a federal budget, and it doesn't have a federal central bank.

There are 17 sovereign states within the eurozone, and 28 within the European Union. Therefore there are 17 or 28 governments, 17 or 28 parliaments, 17 or 28 constitutional courts and, above all, 17 or 28 public opinions.

The protagonists of the financial market normally act in a uniform way, instantaneously. The European states, if they react at all, react in great numbers and therefore slowly, not as one.

To sum up, Europe (still) does not have a single public hand, a hand that in the midst of a crisis can instantaneously and effectively support and/or replace the private hand.

There is a relatively widespread notion that this crisis revolves around hostility the United States holds toward Europe, the hostility that exists between the world of the dollar and the world of the euro. According to this notion, this hostility is based on an American desire for power, a desire to preserve and defend the historic might of the dollar as the world's reserve currency. Why give up this source of strength, from an American point of view? For this reason, it would seem that they are not against the euro but instead in favor of the euro as it has been up until now. In favor, that is, of a strange currency that becomes stronger or weaker against the dollar, not only due to its own merits and faults, but also because, due to structural and constitutional choices, it is a politically neutral currency that can be manipulated from the outside, by the dollar especially. Everything is changing, however, because of the crisis, and the crisis is making it difficult for the euro to maintain its initial oddities. Now the euro must either become a political currency like other currencies or risk failure. For this reason, rather than suspecting and accusing others it is better to understand—and we will come back to this later on—that Europe is harming itself, and could harm others.

But let's look more closely at the second monster. The reality facing Europe is very different from and—I repeat—much more complex than the reality of 2008. First, there was the chain of old banking crises that went unresolved, as well as new, previously undiscovered ones. Second, this time there is also public debt. Europe's public debt expressed in relation to GDP grew quite quickly, because the GDP denominator fell as a result of the crisis. Additionally, a political decision was made to use debt to manage the crisis directly in the theory that this would avert social hardship, stimulate the economy, save the banks and so on. Banking crises combined with an increase in public debt have made, and continue to make, this crisis rise sharply on the scale of systemic risk. Lastly, but most importantly, in Europe there is also an absent and ineffective public hand, or rather, there are so many national public hands, each insufficient on its own, and almost all still operating under the presumption of autonomy. As a result, a huge and chaotic vacuum of power has formed in Europe. That vacuum is all the more dramatic because the crisis is intense, making strong public intervention increasingly necessary. Conversely, it is precisely the growing evidence of political powerlessness that is causing the crisis to spread within and outside Europe. That powerlessness has become an additional critical factor. Not only are Europe's financial foundations in trouble, but the problems in its political foundations are even clearer and even more serious. Europe's problems lie in particular in its constitution, in the European Union Treaty (Maastricht). Those problems are now coming back from its past to bite it, and they are ultimately made even worse by bad policy.

VI
A Stress Test of the European Union Treaties

An international treaty is like a marriage—entered into for better or worse. Well, it now seems that most of the parties to the European Union treaties signed on for the good times based on the spirit of the times when they were signing and didn't give much thought to how they would get through the bad times.

Written before the advent of globalization, the European Union treaties incorporate a dream created when we were still in the age of certainty and stability.

For this reason, their core spirit is positive and progressive. To see this, you need only read the first few articles. They're all about freedom, democracy, equality, human dignity, human rights, well-being, sustainable development, social market economy, the end of divisions, parallel future progress and so on.

Of course, as in all marriages, there is in the European Union treaties a formal provision for bad times that covers certain negative events. These are gathered under the single heading "natural or man-made disaster." Later, this definition is expanded upon to include political risk, armed aggression, war, conflict and economic instability. All these words refer to individual cases and individual states. They are at the same time too specific and conventional and too limited to convey accurately what is happening today.

In short, because of the times and the way they were written, the good and the bad are not given equal air time in the European Union treaties. Rather, the good is the rule, and the bad is the exception.

Meanwhile, over the past few years, to paraphrase Shakespeare, more things have happened on earth than are dreamt of in our philosophy. An impressive cascade of new and negative phenomena have occurred. Two of those have particularly high political intensity: the dramatic geopolitical revolution, moving from the Atlantic toward Asia, destined, among other things, to alter the course of globalization via Mediterranean North Africa, and the even more dramatic economic crisis.

I'm choosing my words carefully here: a *revolution* indicates that all points of reference are overturned; a *crisis* is a form of discontinuity, a paradigm shift.

The major outcome of the original crisis that manifested itself in the American financial sector in 2008, along with a loss of confidence, was a drop in world trade. The crisis consequently pushed many governments in Europe (and the rest of the world) to increase their deficits or public debt, in some cases to guarantee social welfare—meaning the rights peculiar to and typical of the welfare state—and in others to stimulate the economy.

Immediately afterward, many banking and financial structures in Europe crashed. The subsequent public actions undertaken by many European governments to save these structures caused deficits and public debt to grow.

Two essential policy points can be noted in regard to the European Union treaties. Due to either omission or action, these were highly pertinent to the origin as well as the handling of the first phase of the crisis:

1) What was notably missing, early in the crisis, was something expressly mentioned in the European Union treaties: "The cautious vigilance . . . of credit organizations concerning the stability of the financial system." The European Central Bank certainly dealt with inflation, calculated in terms of the cost of a "basket" of goods. Then, with steadfast perseverance, the European Central Bank addressed the question of deficit and public debt.

Yet from the very beginning, in the long years following the launch of the euro, it remained almost mute on the question of credit organizations and private finance, on falling deeper into debt through real estate bubbles and credit cards and so on. It remained completely silent on the risks that could and did derive from the euro's stability. The European banking crisis demonstrates with tangible, absolute and elemental evidence that in Europe the crisis originated in private not public finance, and then private finance was quickly applied to the crisis as if it were medicine rather than being the disease itself.

Basically, the European Central Bank thought and acted as though the stability of the euro, its essential mission, depended only upon levels of inflation or of deficit/public debt and not also on the critical private finance situation, which was not sufficiently monitored, either nationally or centrally, on a macroeconomic level. Credit organizations and private finance were free to fall apart as they were completely ignored, unobserved, left unmonitored. They were not on the European Central Bank's radar screen, again, not even at the macroeconomic level, which was and is its area of expertise. This probably happened because at that time, private finance was widely agreed to be incapable of making any mistakes.

In reality, the lesson of this crisis is that the risk was not only a question of excessive public debt, but also and above all, a question of excessive private debt. It is perhaps in an effort to mask its old mistakes that the European Central Bank is now blaming governments for not imposing sanctions on Germany and France for having excessive public deficits in 2003, forgetting that the crisis did not begin here, with unmonitored deficits and public debt (in 2007, Ireland's public debt was minimal, about 25%; Portugal's was about 63%), but instead came from private difficulties that went undetected or ignored.

2) On the other hand, after 2008 and almost as if to compensate for this mistake, much more was done. In the wording of the treaties, a crisis was and is in fact only

recognized with reference to particular events ("serious difficulties in the provision of certain products, especially within the energy sector") or with reference only to individual states: "serious turmoil in the economic life of a member state"; "in case one member state finds itself in difficulty or is seriously threatened by serious natural difficulties, or exceptional circumstances beyond its control."

There is a reason for this. The treaties were based on *ex ante* logic, aimed at creating a common market. This type of logic is derived from individual states considered to be separate. The crisis, on the other hand, happened a few decades later on a systemic global scale, and in a market that in turn was already created, aggregated and consolidated as a system. This required that the crisis be handled, and/or did not prevent the crisis from being handled, with strong political determination that went beyond the wording of the treaties. It was clear that this crisis needed to be evaluated and handled as what it was: a systemic crisis within the market.

It is in this scenario and under these terms that the conventional European paradigm was inverted. This happened on a macro as well as a micro level. Before the crisis, there were public finance obligations on the macro level, and on the micro level state intervention was prohibited. Since the crisis, public finance obligations have been removed on the macro level, while the prohibition on state intervention has also been removed on the micro level.

Today, however, it is glaringly obvious that this type of broad and evolutionary interpretation of the treaties is no longer sufficient. At this point, the treaties themselves are no longer sufficient. Today's systemic intensity, so redolent of the crisis, calls for a different, more effective range of interventions. Such interventions are not easy to impose, however, in light of Europe's history.

VII
A Stroll Through European History

In order to understand what's happening, and what could happen, in Europe, all you need to do is take a look at the historical-political map.

We'll look closely at three key points on this map: Waterloo (the site of Napoleon's final battle), Westphalia (the place where, after the Augsburg Settlement, the principle of *cuius regio, eius religio*, or "whose realm, his religion," meaning that a ruler could impose his religion on the people, was firmly established) and Versailles (where Germany's reparations were decided upon).

I begin with a question: Was Waterloo a victory or a defeat for Europe? It was certainly a victory for England and therefore for the new world of the Atlantic. Symmetrically, it was a defeat for the old world of continental Europe—its first defeat, after the first instance of globalization.

It was certainly an avoidable defeat, for Napoleon's forces wielded not only pagan strength and Jacobin spirit, but also the learning of the Enlightenment, backed by a Christian humanism that led even Voltaire to describe Europe as a "grande république." A grande république at once very old and very new, with a great, common and unbeatable foundation of religion, culture, principles, values and law. As Machiavelli first described it, a free land, as opposed to Asia, which was dominated by despotism.

But let's return to the present: Does an idea of Europe as a great republic still make sense? Is it still useful?

It certainly is, because globalization tends to reduce the weight and role of the old European nation-states. It also tends to enlarge the scale and fashion itself into a new archipelago made up of masses of continental blocks, while competition and opposition between those blocks continue to grow.

In this scenario, what is Europe's purpose, what are its positive and negative chances? We shall answer this by moving to the second place in our history, Westphalia.

Westphalia is, after the Augsburg Settlement, the definitive home of the *cuius regio, eius religio* principle, the origin of Europe's particular cultures and varying national spirits. It is here that the largest and most critical of Europe's current paradoxes emerges.

Nationalism has all but disappeared from every part of Europe. It has disappeared from culture and music, from habits of consumption and customs, yet it lives on and—almost in retaliation—is becoming more radical, maintaining its nucleus of resistance in one strategic place: the public budgets of the states.

Of course, the political relevance of the public

budgets should not be downplayed. A public budget reflects the vices and virtues of the population. Yet it is simply impossible for everything—the size and structure not only of the economy but of our lives, our past, present, future—to be reduced to and measured in economic spreads or interest rates paid on bonds of public debt in one day, in a bidding war, without the slightest economic analysis or sense of historical perspective. Countries that are now doing well were doing very badly only a few years ago. All countries can see their fates upset or reversed, from positive to negative, and in a short space of time, because now everything depends on everybody.

With the crisis, the age of deficit spending in Europe is at an end. A country's fortune lies in the balance and order of its public budget. The budget offers guaranteed social cohesion, the ability to gain capital by spending less than others and becoming stronger than others, prestige due to good practices. But this is only one point of view. And policy cannot be evaluated seriously in chunks of one year or a few years. Longer historical periods are needed so that a more complete group of facts and data, both positive and negative, can be collected. The reality of the relationship between states is usually much more complex than the information that can be drawn from a budget covering one year or a few years. That leads us to our third historical destination: Versailles.

The story of the reparations imposed on Germany begins in Versailles in 1919. This obtuse notion was conceived of by a victorious France and was devised in order to allow its war with Germany to continue to be fought on the battlefield of economics.

Today, we should carefully avoid employing similar punitive austerity measures. Otherwise, a new, reverse Versailles may be imposed vengefully by Germany on the rest of Europe. Perhaps it's time to create a budget that is as broad and balanced as possible. To start, it should be noted that almost everyone benefited, first from the European Union, and then from the euro. Germany gained unification and opened up huge new swaths of the market. France injected its history into Europe, promoted its tradition of international politics and fiercely protected its agricultural industry. Italy buried its enormous public debt deep in the fortress of Maastricht. And so on, country by country.

In any case, no country can now claim to be able to save itself independently, to be able to create alone a budget "with benefit of inventory." There is no sense in pretending. We can't suddenly decide to forget the advantages, interests and gains achieved in the past, or the prospects for the future, both positive and negative. Whoever benefited earlier on, selling many of their products as well as the debt that was necessary to buy them, cannot be allowed to forget that. We cannot now progress by means of protectionism or national egotism. All you need to do is read the economic and financial map of Europe to understand the degree of integration that exists and to realize that there are no longer any national problems, and that therefore national solutions are no longer necessary.

We should note first that the European Common Market was and is made up of real as well as financial exchanges. With this dual nature, it is a market structured on a vast scale, with highly reciprocal density.

Let's begin with the real exchanges. A highly complex shared trade network of goods and services stretches across Europe from country to country. The most common type of export in Europe today is not external export, but instead Europe to Europe export. More than 60% of German, French and Italian exports are made to other European countries, including the so-called "peripheral" countries (Greece, Ireland, Portugal, etc.).[14]

And now the financial exchanges. The same holds true here: These are mainly Europe to Europe transactions. The only difference is these exchanges are not evenly distributed, as is obvious from their concentration, along with their associated risks, in core Europe (Germany, France, etc.) To give an idea, the Bank for International Settlements has just estimated the exposure of British, French, German and Benelux banks to Greece, Ireland, Portugal and Spain, including derivatives, at about 2.5 trillion dollars in the period ending September 30, 2010. The German portion totals 568.6 billion, the French part is 440.4 and the United Kingdom's share comes to 431. British banks are particularly

[14] Further details can be found in Appendix 9.

exposed to Ireland, to the tune of 225 billion dollars, and Spain with 152 billion. French banks, meanwhile, are exposed by 224.7 billion dollars to Spain and by 92 billion dollars to Greece. German banks are exposed by 208 billion dollars to Ireland and 242 billion dollars to Spain. The Benelux countries are exposed by 189 billion to Spain, while the Spanish banks are exposed by 109 billion to Portugal.[15]

Obviously, this is a heavily and systematically interconnected environment where a crisis could cause these risks to blow up in a sort of chain reaction, as in an economic and political atomic meltdown.

At a certain point, it seemed as if, by magic, we'd take the right path. Under the pressure of the crisis, with political awareness of the common relationships and common risks at play, we'd make the right choice. The first steps were taken along that path. That was Europe's last great political moment. And then everything changed.

[15] Further details can be found in Appendix 10.

VIII
May's Great Illusion and the Deauville Autumn

Flash back to the weekend of May 7 to 10, 2010.

First, there was a meeting of the Extraordinary Council of European Heads of State and Governments in Brussels on May 7. Then, from May 9 to May 10, an Extraordinary Ecofin Council meeting.

During the night between May 9 and May 10, before the dawn brought a common and positive solution, all kinds of things were happening.

There were those who were assuming that this was the end of the euro as a common currency. They knew a little secret and were therefore carefully and quietly thinking up national identification codes to be stamped on euro banknotes: Z for Belgium, X for Germany, V for Spain, U for France, S for Italy, R for Luxembourg, P for the Netherlands. Some were considering closing their banks for the night and applying special ink so that the national codes on the euro banknotes inside those banks could be corrected.

In other words, at least initially, the idea of printing new national currency was ruled out. It was expected that it would be sufficient to continue to use the old euro banknotes, albeit with the help of a few special tricks. They simply would no longer function as a common currency, but instead would form new national currencies.

Then, just when it seemed like it was already too late, the right solution was found. At the dawn of the next day and over the following three months, a new political architecture began to take shape in Europe. Our common destiny was not to be terminated by crisis.

To understand how new this architecture was on our economic and political landscape, look at Europe as it was before and compare it to what took shape that day at dawn.

Before the crisis, Europe was a geographical continent, a common market with a common currency, but it did not have true, common economic and political governance.

After the crisis, under pressure, a new European architecture began to take shape, beginning that weekend in May. An architecture that was more political than economic, based on four pillars: the European Central Bank; the European Financial Stability Facility; the then-new Stability and Growth Pact; and the subsequent common policy of financial responsibility.

The first two pillars were conceived of as an *external* defense. The second two pillars were to serve an *internal* disciplinary function. Let's examine them in detail.

The external defense:

a) The first pillar of external defense was the new defensive function entrusted to the European Central Bank, which from then on was *politically* authorized to buy European bonds on the secondary market, to protect them from speculation;

b) The second pillar of external defense, the European Financial Stability Facility, destined to become Europe's new monetary fund, had the same defensive role as the European Central Bank but greater flexibility. At its heart was the spirit of Roosevelt's Lend-Lease law, which financed the arming of the United Kingdom during the war against Nazism: If your neighbor's house is burning, you'd better lend him your extinguisher. There was also the added possibility of making the European Financial Stability Facility a vehicle for issuing Eurobonds in the future.

Internal discipline:

c) The third pillar, upon which internal discipline was to be based, was the new Stability and Growth Pact, set out according to three criteria: a coordinated budget session, supervision and sanctions for noncompliant countries. The coordinated budget session was considered a can't-miss appointment.

Indeed, it would see the introduction of a strong, highly political idea of a devolution of powers, from the states to Europe.

Oversight had to be strengthened, and it had to be extended to cover private finance and all the big critical issues, from household debt to pensions.

Real and effective sanctions would be imposed against noncompliant countries, and they would be economic sanctions, not just political ones.

d) Finally, the fourth pillar: budget discipline.

This pillar is not only economic, but also political and somewhat ideological as well: The conviction that a policy of responsibility should be enacted in all of the countries. The continent of Europe now produces more debt than wealth and has more deficit than gross domestic product.

Together, the announcement and initial implementation of this political architecture, of this more united and cohesive Europe, were enough to convey a positive message to the outside world and the financial market. That message was most definitely economic, but it was also strongly political. Immediately after the announcement, European spreads began to move in a positive direction.

It was obvious to everyone during those extraordinary days that the political component was much more important than the economic one.

Rather than a huge, instantaneous and real commitment of capital (at the beginning the estimate was limited to about 700 billion euros), what was significant was the attempt to deter speculation, but also perhaps even more importantly the new message conveyed by the European Union by means of this commitment to new mutual political and economic action. This had a huge impact on confidence in European bonds.

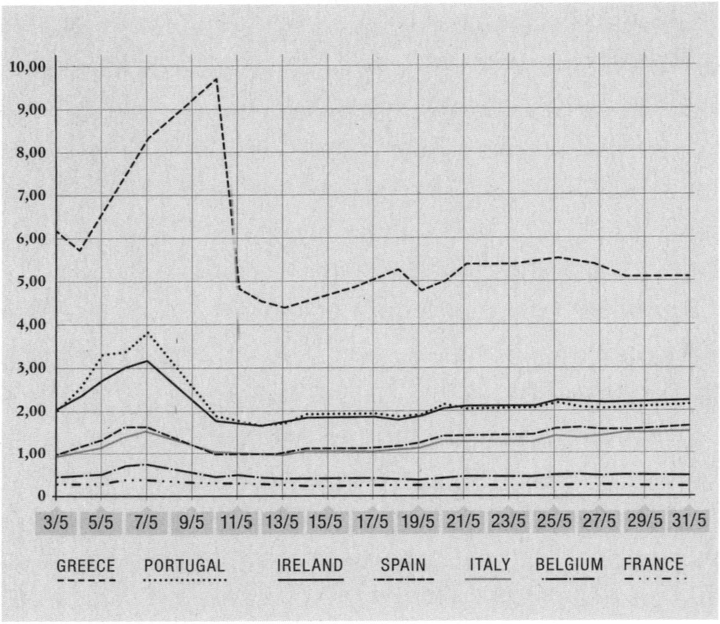

Fig. 7. Ten-year spreads in relation to the Bund in May 2010.

At that time, international finance appeared more united than divided. For the first time, the European governments were beginning to be more united than divided, too.

This was the last great illusion. The illusion of constructing a future in Europe that would not be negative, but positive, and of constructing at its heart a new common political purpose.

Then, unfortunately, spring turned to autumn. After that, everything changed. And not for the better. In autumn, a radically contradictory message was issued from Deauville, a typical belle époque resort town. The leaders of Germany and France had met to declare that a sovereign signature, similar to a government's signature on its bonds, could be recognized as a private signature, and as such it could be withdrawn or not honored. This could be handled using certain private sector–derived insolvency clauses. Buyers of public bonds would not be guaranteed a return. The risk that until then had been reserved for the private sector was extended to the public sector, so that this latter sector became, in turn, privatized.

Over the course of history, the normal sequence has gone as follows: first, the state becomes unstable, then comes the announcement of how it is to be managed. Commitments are reduced—known as taking a haircut—or renounced entirely.

At Deauville, the sequence was reversed: First came the media announcement of a political plan in the possible event of public default, then came the consequences. In the middle of a credit crisis involving not only the banks but also the states, nobody remembered or appreciated the fact that the word credit comes from the Latin *credere*—to believe.

There is a type of crisis that in turn generates further crisis, when not only does finance not believe in finance, but states don't believe in states.

The first thing that happened after the Deauville message was disseminated was that the idea of kicking

Greece out of the eurozone began to be discussed . That's pretty odd if one considers that all the euro banknotes contain a word written in Greek.

Just the announcement of this possibility provided the opportunity for speculation. Ireland collapsed only a few weeks later.

The European summit of December 16 to 17, 2010, partially and confusedly corrected the message of Deauville.

This is how Europe fell into the trap of borrowing. It built that trap for itself, though. Because just the idea of a total or partial private enterprise insolvency clause or a partial guarantee not only divides the public bond market, but causes all related interest rates on the market to rise. When major risks are officially announced, an investor may continue to invest, but he will always charge higher interest if he does.

To sum up, chaos was created as a result of ignoring the two essential lessons that the crisis had taught us: First, that counterparty risk automatically shifts the default of a business or bank incorporated in one country onto the counterparty business or bank in another country. Indeed, even if we still maintain the old political boundaries in Europe, we have removed all the other boundaries, starting with the economic ones. Secondly, that private debts can infect public debts and vice versa. And from one subject to another, from one system to another, from one state to another, the contagion spreads like wildfire, from private banking systems to public budgets. Following this path, it can destroy not just economic and social structures, but people's lives.

The political duty to be strict with public budgets must be paramount, for all the states, in all the states: strictness in the management and reduction of old public debts, as well as strictness in avoiding new ones in the future.

But it is delusional to believe that the cost generated by a crisis can remain limited to the individual state where the crisis began. In a shipwreck, you aren't safe just because you're traveling in first class.

And yet, in the European political theater, this irrationally limited vision still persists, beyond any logic, even after Deauville, and the official word is that it will not be discussed any further.

It was at Deauville in particular that the ghosts of the past emerged together and cast a shadow over the future. It was then that all the negative characteristics particular to Europe's contemporary politics emerged: not only the excessive power exerted by finance on politics, but also, and worse, the way any remaining European political power is wasted through horizontal indecision.

IX
Europe?!

Europe appeared to us for at least twenty years as the construction site for a new and futuristic positive political system. The changes made to classic political forms were new and forward-thinking and positive. The process of combining the old nation-states into a union was new, forward-thinking and positive. All of this now risks crumbling into a pile of rubble.

Why? Because for at least twenty years, politics in Europe has contracted out its work to the economy, which in turn subcontracted this work first to the market and then to the financial market.

This is why Europe today finds itself surrounded on all sides by borderline crazy anomalies. Today, in a dramatic crescendo of experience and evidence, it is becoming more and more clear that in Europe we have:

– A real crisis, but a fake central bank;

– A currency without states, but also states without a currency;

– A crisis that is passing directly from one of currency to one of politics, after politics made itself over in the image of the economy, an economy that was in turn contained within currency;

– A currency without government that transforms democracy into an unprecedented government of currency.

These four anomalies must be examined more closely.

A Real Crisis, But a Fake Central Bank

Europe has a common currency, but it doesn't have a common central bank, and consequently, in the midst of a crisis such as this one, it is almost as if there weren't a common currency. Unlike the old European central banks, and unlike the other central banks of the world—the Federal Reserve in the United States, the Bank of Japan, the Bank of China, the Bank of England and so on—the European Central Bank has some monetary functions, for example control of inflation, but it doesn't have the primary and typical function of a true central bank: the mission of an agent of government, the mission of being the lender of last resort. A guarantor within the system, of the system and for the system. This function was first introduced in a very different and remote historical context, in 1694 with the Bank of England.

This anomalous and imbalanced arrangement makes the European Central Bank very different from other central banks. It was of little relevance before the crisis and/or in the absence of crisis, as long as gambling on perpetual peaceful development in Europe continued to work. That was when there was everything to gain and nothing to lose, nothing to risk. Today, the European Central Bank's limited function is highly relevant. Within a crisis of the sort now taking place, a real central bank needs to have powers sufficient to prevent liquidity problems from transforming into solvency problems. These are vital powers, especially when it is not only a part of a banking system, or even an entire banking system at stake, but instead the state, or several states. It should be noted that it is almost always unnecessary for a bank truly to intervene in a liquidity-solvency crisis. Announcing that the bank is ready to take steps usually does the trick. That's enough to cut off attempts at speculation. Why? Because no private entity has as much money at its disposal as a central bank does. Furthermore, even if speculation could mobilize a sufficient (enormous) amount of money, it would not be able to get past the central bank, because it would immediately lose a part of its total, given that printing money, a.k.a. quantitative easing, brings with it the risk of inflation and therefore the risk of losses for the investor, who might buy an item at 100, but who, as a result of a drop in the value of money caused by public intervention and then inflation, could suddenly find himself with *100–x*, where *x* is normally greater than the profit from speculation.

None of this is the case in Europe, however. Of course, the European Central Bank is situated in Frankfurt, but this was evidently not considered and still is not considered enough of a guarantee. On the contrary, anything approaching the idea of a true common currency that's handled and managed jointly (which does not include the euro as it is now) is met with diffidence. In short, all the European states decided to give up their own currencies, but they also gave up the idea of creating a true European currency to be managed and handled on behalf of the individual states by a central bank. Without a central bank, with the honeymoon over and the crisis in full swing, it is increasingly obvious that the limited function of the European Central Bank lends the euro itself limited credibility. Like Byzantium's ancient nongold issue currency, the euro appears to be a quasi-currency.

As a result of all this, in Europe, under the pressure created by the crisis and ever more quickly over the last year, what was supposed to be done was not done. Instead, something that should not have been done was done. Between the events of Deauville and now, time has been wasted, sparking various, confusing alternative strategies. Three erroneous types of intervention were performed and are still underway this year.[16]

[16] For further information on the three erroneous types of intervention that were carried out one after the other following the events at Deauville, see Appendix 11.

A Currency Without States and States Without a Currency

There are numerous mysteries and legends surrounding the creation of the euro. With both the passage of time and the intensification of the crisis, they are gradually being revealed, beginning with the secrets and mysterious codes that surround the unification of Germany.

What is well established is that the euro is a continental currency and as such should principally reflect the continental foundations of the unified economy underlying it. But is that true? To be sure, we would need to respond to the following question: Why at the time of the creation of the euro, on January 1, 1999, was one euro worth about 1.16 dollars and now it is worth 1.30?

What happened? Has the euro gotten stronger while the dollar weakened, due to real differences in their respective underlying economic foundations, or is there an artificial effect behind the euro due to the fact that, unlike the dollar, the euro is purposefully not a political currency? As a passive rather than an active currency, it can abandon the battlefield to the currency that competes against it.

In any case, the euro is structurally a continental currency and not a national one, with a single exchange rate. It does not reflect the economic foundations of the individual nation-states. This status was highlighted further by the way those nation-states diverged and grew out of proportion to one another after it was created, and now that those differences have been amplified further by the crisis, the euro can even seem a bit like an alien currency. Alien, and also hostile. *Rebus sic stantibus* (things thus standing), hostile because of its rigid, invariable and inflexible exchange rate and above all because, due to the way it is structurally organized, it deprives the individual states of the tools needed to handle a real crisis. Those tools are inaccessible because of how the euro and the European Central Bank are structured. And they are not to be found underlying it, either, because the states don't have their own currencies and central banks. Perhaps it would be beneficial to have a true central bank and a true European currency, not so that they can opportunistically devalue themselves, but so that they can defend themselves.

In short, the tools needed to manage a structural, fundamental and dramatic crisis such as this one are missing in Europe. These tools did exist in Europe before the introduction of the euro, and they still do in rest of the world. Those in the rest of the West and in Asia have stopped investing, or at least are investing less in stocks and bonds denominated in euros because they can't understand this almost suicidal structure. In response, Europeans sometimes say, "If you don't believe in us, why should we believe in ourselves?" This is why we need a real European central bank—to conserve instead of to wear down the euro. And then we need Eurobonds, for very good reasons that will be set out later.

Of course, in Europe the states must and can introduce increasingly austere figures in their public budgets. There is no alternative but to be more rigorous. Globalization has ended the age of deficit spending. Yet austerity measures, while necessary, are not necessarily the best medicine. If the crisis is not handled with new currency maneuvers, public budgets will destabilize. As a result, cost of debt will rise so that it becomes unmanageable. At this terminal stage, crisis in turn creates crisis, and the situation is aggravated until, finally, the states are caught in a destructive spiral.

Europe and the Economy

Originally, the fortunes of Europe were based on the so-called Monnet method, on the idea of inventing politics with economics. The theory goes something like, *federate their portfolios and you will federate their hearts*. But now it's gone too far. Europe is not a political structure that has an economy. Europe is rather an economy that has designed and distorted a political structure in its image. It wasn't like that at the start, in the initial heroic phase of principles and values. It wasn't like that a long while ago, in the phase of the ECM, or European Common Market. A common market between separate and real nation-states. The environment was still too nationalistic and not common enough, not European enough, but at least politics still prevailed over economics. The bankers were denied entry and not even allowed into the waiting room. Everything changed, and not all for the better, when the fall of the Berlin Wall and German reunification made it possible for the era of the euro to begin. The era of currency, the primary driving force in Europe's latest evolution. The euro was a currency that had been in the works for a while. This is why it could immediately be introduced, playing off the fast pace of history that had started with the fall of the Berlin Wall. Fast action was taken with the aim of avoiding a global crisis. The currency was therefore put into circulation using friction to start it up, as if the euro were an old car whose engine had to be cranked to spark. The market, concentrated and sublimated into this currency, suddenly slipped in and replaced politics. For its part, politics voluntarily and progressively put itself first at the disposal of the market and then at the disposal of the financial market, both in the old nation-states and in the new nation-states that had been given ad hoc power.

Just as in the rest of the world, in Europe nobody realized what was happening, and nobody suffered any consequences while everything was going well. It was only due to the crisis that the idea began to surface that politics is more and more about the economy. It was only because of the crisis that the myth of the all-knowing market began to die.

But now we need politics. The absence of politics is hurting us on both a national and a European level. The image of politics these days is of large, repetitive and endless European meetings that have begun to resemble those disastrous meetings of the League of Nations between the wars. The only meeting after the meeting in May 2010 that was slightly different was the December 8 to 9, 2011, meeting. But we'll come back to that later. What's important to understand here is that this is how European governments, afraid of losing elections and afraid of having their credit ratings downgraded, have handily managed to pull off the great achievement of having both of those things happen.

A Currency Without a Government and a Government Without a Currency

The final battlefield will be—and is—democracy. All the European states are indeed formally democratic. Democratic in the classic sense of the term. But all of them are beginning to lose vast parts of their original and individual democracies. For a start, like all the nation states of the world, the European nation states are ceding democratic powers to the market, which cannot exactly be defined as a new alternative form of democracy. Only fanatics believe that. It's disproved by the simple fact that the people who get ahead in the market are the people with the most money. Moreover, unlike the other nation-states of the world, the European nation-states are now undergoing an intense, new and typically European process of devolving upward, meaning that they are ceding jurisdictions and powers to European institutions, such as the European Commission, the European Council, the European Court and the European Central Bank. In the past, those jurisdictions and powers were controlled and enforced by national democracies. These European institutions, for their part, do not always fit the parameters, criteria, models and principles of classic democracy. We tend to say, rather optimistically, that the democratic aspect of all of these institutions is still mostly in the experimental phase, still in the process of being established.

However, the crisis put pressure on and then blew up this entire arrangement.

There is a rising political risk in all of this, and it's growing as the crisis continues. It's the risk that there will be abuse of a state of emergency and dominant para-democratic and technocratic institutions will invade the territory of classic democracy. These institutions are capable of doing so. That is a fact in our times, as we live in an era that is predominantly economic and are seeing the primacy of politics replaced with the primacy of economics. The supposedly strictly confidential letter that the European Central Bank sent to the Bank of Italy and the Italian government on August 5, 2011, is an obvious example of this. It is a letter full of financial doctrine, containing a government program expressly prepared by a monetary authority for a political authority. It offers deadlines and details for compulsory and detailed action, scheduled to the minute. This action seems more executive than parliamentary. There is the threat—inferred but never quite spelled out—of aid being withdrawn from Italy. Aid that would take the form of acquisitions of Italian public bonds on the secondary market. A form of aid which, as discussed in Appendix 11, is of questionable technical use. What matters here, however, are the political rather than the economic facts. The type of demands and ultimatums made in the letter by the European Central Bank and the Bank of Italy are normally made by the International Monetary Fund. Yet this organization—even if it is very aggressive, barely democratic and pretty unlucky, an organization that bears the stigma of global doom—is at least totally transparent, because it says that it can intervene, and then tells you what you have to do. The European Central Bank and the Bank of Italy operate in the dark. They say they can't do what they in fact can—and do—do, and they use this power politically and selectively, on the condition that you don't go blabbing about it to everyone.

Basically, in Europe democracy is becoming increasingly less national and increasingly weak. It has been eroded from below, on a national level, but has not been made cohesive on the higher, European level. There is a risk that at a time of crisis this will have destructive effects.

To be clear: At one time, the military had the say-so over a state of emergency. The military took over radio and television stations and imposed nighttime curfews, or whatever it felt needed to be done. Today, in the postmodern version, an emergency situation is declared based on the systemic performance of the euro, with a related charge possibly made against a certain country for having caused the failure of the euro system, as if this system would otherwise have been quite stable. A state of emergency is enacted by conditioning and commissioning governments and parliaments, experimenting with the new so-called reinforced European governance. It is finance that announces the state of emergency, imposing its own government. People wearing the universal financial uniform; technocrat apostles; Utopian enthusiasts, still convinced of market dogma; applied economics engineers, as in the Politburo before the fall of Communism; totalitarian clones of Saint-Simon are making these decisions. Actually, this type of culture can be useful. But not on its own—only when it's combined with other cultures and sensibilities. It can't just be the authors of a disaster who return to the site where the disaster erupted. The tools normally used are disruptive, preemptive manipulations of the financial market. The message transmitted to the people is one of a strong injunction, an injunction so strong that nobody, neither states nor citizens, can refuse to play along, if not at their own risk. And so fear spreads. There is a kind of daytime curfew and distressing urgent messages are transmitted about spreads, about interest rate differentials that have risen sharply at the expense of target states. Interest rates become an alternative means for implementing policy. The goal is to force a parliament holiday, in place of a bank holiday. An old democratic government that shuts its doors can then potentially be replaced with a new, less democratic one. In this way, democracy in Europe is not only weakened by the excess of internal inequalities, where the rich grow richer and the poor grow poorer, but it is also subject to new external pressures, and it has already lost some of its old national sovereignty. What we have seen in Europe in some states is only the beginning of what will—if we fail to resist—take the form of a growing shift of power away from republican democracy. It will end in an unwritten *Ermächtigungsgesetz*, a law giving full emergency powers dreamed up by Carl Schmitt. This will result in a state of emergency and a new form of fascism—financial fascism, white-collar fascism.

I feel compelled to add that it's not that there aren't any problems, it's just that this is the wrong solution to them. Precisely because there are problems, this cannot be the solution. However, there is another possible solution, which will be discussed in the following pages.

X
Germany?!

The crisis is also so very serious in Europe due to an external reason: The United States no longer plays a guiding role in the world. Of course, the financial powers that be are still largely American, and American culture, ideology, language and capital are pervasive in the financial markets.

But the United States no longer has enough political power to impose a general, structural design on the world, as it did at Bretton Woods in 1944. Ultimately, it doesn't even have enough power to suggest or impose fitting solutions to a crisis such as this one.

If the United States is absent from the world stage, and if Europe is absent from Europe, then not even Germany can fix the situation all by itself.

Even the new Germany, the leader of the Franco-German axis, the center of old Europe that deserves to be the center of new Europe isn't up to the task.

The new Europe has become intergovernmental, supergovernmental even. It's very different from the old Europe, which was based on the community method.

Of course, the privileged bilateral relationship between Germany and France has been there from the very beginning. Yet it was just a part of the political economy typical of the community mechanism and not the entire thing. This community mechanism was not hierarchical, but truly representative of a community. It struck an appropriate balance between different interests, the individual motives of large and small, strong and weak, long-standing and new member states. It did this within an arbitrage system, under the direction of common European institutions: the Council, the Commission, the Parliament and so on. It was run with one goal in mind, and that was a general and not an individual goal of serving the interests of the union.

Now everything is different, and this difference leads us to evaluate the pros and cons inherent in this new organization. In doing so, it becomes obvious that everything goes back to the enigma that is Germany, and the crisis that shrouds it in mystery. You cannot now be in favor of Europe, or a true friend to Germany, unless you have compared and weighed the various positive and negative viewpoints, as set out below.

Germany: Pros

The first pro is that Germany has performed very well, both in handling its own reunification and in restructuring its industrial system in response to globalization.

Today it is the only European economy that actually works. The second pro lies in the extraordinary cultural vitality of Germany, evident, for example, in its schools of philosophy. The third and most important reason lies in its culture of stability. Obviously the anguish of the past instilled a fear of return to the hyperinflation and subsequent monetary breakdown of the Weimar era, which also had terrible social effects. That brought about today's positive culture. And at the root of this culture there is also a need to safeguard the future against the mistakes of the past. That need is perfectly suited to the spirit of our times. This is a fundamental political fact.

The times we live in are marked by the effective end of the colonial age and consequently by the end of leverage in relation to deficit spending. But as of the end of World War II, that kind of spending had been used to enact modern social policies. Well-being bought on credit. We can't do that anymore, because we can no longer sustain a public deficit that is higher than GDP. So we all must, and we all will, be forced to acquire increasing amounts of this culture of stability. That's not because this culture is German, but because there are no other alternatives that can secure our future.

If I were in a joking mood or in the mood to stir up controversy, I might call that reverence for stability a national characteristic typical of Germany. It could also be said that in addition to exporting goods to Europe, Germany is also imposing its own cultural and structural reforms on Europe. These days, everything must be German. But that's not all that's at work here. At the heart of the culture of stability are not only fears from the past but also the needs that we have forced on ourselves in the present. These are times better suited to ants than to grasshoppers. Yet it is precisely for this reason that we find it so difficult to understand and to participate in the means to reach the ends, meaning stability. The current policy in Europe, modeled after Germany, does not produce stability, but instead produces its exact opposite. This policy is being developed through the accumulation of various and diverse factors, real and potential factors, moving and inert, marginal and lethal factors that have been revolving for about a year within Germany and producing an effect that is the exact opposite of stability: serious and progressive instability.

Germany: Cons

It has long been said that Germany has enormous virtues and very few faults, but at a certain point it always uses its virtues in the service of its few faults. So it does have some negatives, which are set out below:

a) The Franco-German axis began to fray soon after German unification, as was already evident at the time. It could be seen in the way differences over foreign policy played out, as well as differences over the European budget, over expansion and referendums and more. But now, in this time of crisis, this discord is more significant than ever.

Now the Franco-German axis maintains a mutually beneficial relationship that hides France's weakness and disguises Germany's strength. Strictly through the law of numbers, the old Franco-German pair has finally been replaced by a German quasimonarchy. Rather than the two countries forming a bilateral axis, Germany wears the pants.

b) In a move that was once believed impossible after the centuries-old game of mutual loathing, opposition and war, a new, huge trading market has been created within Germany, eastward and northward. This is a kind of internal market created with funds from European finance, productive outsourcing and an import-export flow. Through expansion and by means of investments and commerce, true German protectorates have been established: Here is a market inside the core of the common market. For almost a decade, rumors flew in Europe that the push for continuous expansion (the newest member of the European Union is Croatia, which joined in December 2011) was a perfidious Anglo-Saxon plot, an anti-European plot to dilute the central political nucleus of Europe in a great sea of countries. In reality, it seems clear today that all of this was nonsense.

Germany had another reason to support the eastward expansion. Using commercial and regional logic, it saw a way to create an internal market for itself. This allows it to regain, with interest, the German investment in the European budget. The European budget is indeed the source of the generous contributions made to these new member countries, contributions that are funded by everyone but are capitalized on mostly by their German neighbors.

c) The European budget. Let's just say that, in the give and take of the budget, and contrary to what has been said, Germany certainly hasn't done too badly in this area.

Without a doubt Germany makes the largest net contribution to the European Union. It provides 5.9 billion euros, ahead of France, which gives 5.2, and Italy, which gives 4.2. This is only due to the size of its population, however. Considered not by national population, but per capita, a more "European" way of looking at things, France and Italy are ahead of Germany. Counting Germany as the top contributor is supported neither by the figures, nor by the spirit of the European Union.

d) We should add to this the massive and active geopolitical game being played in a northeasterly direction, toward Russia. All of this together represents a geoeconomic imbalance, but more importantly a geopolitical imbalance. All of this makes Europe imbalanced. It seems to be concrete proof of the theory that Germany is too big for Europe, both because of its makeup and because of its position.

e) Located around Germany are states with their own individual electoral and political histories that involved all kinds of alliances and hostilities. Those states use their individual powers of veto in different, sometimes conflicting ways. They all like to sing a solo in the spotlight every once in a while. This usually takes the form of picking things apart to the point of ridiculousness. The most recent example of this was Finland requesting what came to be called "Finnish collateral," i.e., guarantees on the loans to Greece that only Finland would receive, a move clearly based on politics rather than economics. And yet, while they differ wildly in many ways, when they need to, they can all, from the north to the east, join the chorus and belt out Germany's tune.

f) The crisis has been handled poorly in the past year, with continual vetoes and unilateral blocks that were often reflections of national egotism, as well as electoral weakness. This has all worked out very nicely for Germany. There are two reasons for that, and they're actually two sides of the same coin.

The first reason is political: The crisis has provided grounds for forcefully implementing Germany's culture of stability in politics. That isn't bad in and of itself, but it's been mishandled. Rather than doing the right thing and promoting the culture described above as a general guiding principle and the only true and right way to conduct European politics, we ceded to the temptation to impose it on everyone, treating it as if it were just another of Germany's exports. This has kept Germany a political powerhouse. One example of this is that if a European Financial Stability Facility intervention becomes necessary, the European Commission will transmit the confidential documents of other countries to the budget committee of the Bundestag.

The second reason is economic. External instability usually comes in the form of the euro and the way the euro is organized (meaning it has no central bank) damaging countries other than Germany. In other words, the greater internal stability caused by the euro situation brings low-cost capital to Germany. In this scenario, the balance of the (not always avoidable) weaknesses of other countries and Germany's own virtues is a positive one for Germany. This financial dumping, resulting from a mix of calculation and chance, allows Germany to increase its investments—both foreign investments in Germany and German investments abroad. By financing itself this way, Germany is able to resolve its own internal issues. It can acquire external banks that have been destabilized precisely because of the European stress tests imposed on them and are therefore very attractively priced. Moreover, Germany can participate in European privatization programs imposed throughout Europe through so-called "recovery policies" and the like.

The result is that a new type of economic expansion is now arriving on the scene, and it can be analyzed under the civil war theory.[17]

[17] "Perhaps no longer as in 1939–1945, but we can still create war using economic levers" (Jacques Delors, 2011). For more on the idea of civil war and on the postmodern movement from conventional war to commercial competition, see G. Tremonti, *La guerra 'civile'* ("Civil" War), Il Mulino, 1996, pp. 842–856.

This type of economic policy confuses short-term opportunistic vision with more far-sighted vision. This type of policy does have some staying power, and it can certainly be driven to the limits, but in doing so, it will create a perilous risk—for Germany in particular—of things going into a tailspin. It's all a big game of chicken. The cars are speeding headlong toward each other, and everyone's waiting to see which driver will give in and swerve first. There is one caveat here, however. When interest rates rise, as they will sooner or later, Germans and anyone who has invested in German bonds at practically zero interest will see the value of their investments drop drastically. This will have disastrous results on balance sheets and is yet another scenario that could force crisis upon crisis.

g) Also, in recent years the Kombinat of industry and banking in Germany has signed a Mephistophelian pact with the rest of Europe: While being virtuous at home (not really, if you consider the obscure and distinctly nonvirtuous activities typical of some of the large German banks and major local banks), Germany has invested its capital in nonvirtuous, peripheral Europe. Fuelled by its own interests, Germany has gone to the dark side to finance demand for German products—such as German cars—in those countries. But it has also done this due to the high interest rates provided as a reward for the risk. Nonvirtuous countries offered those interest rates to the virtuous ones, which were so interested in balancing their internal deficits using the super yields that they accepted the offer. After all, behind every happy debtor there is a happy creditor. What will happen to these debtors and creditors if the European crisis comes to a dramatic head?

In conclusion, while Germany was forced to exchange its deutsche marks for reunification, now, at the close of a twenty-year historical cycle, many people think and fear that the euro is being remade in the image of the old deutsche mark. Germany has a pattern of undergoing tremendous change every twenty years. Count back twenty years, and you are at the time of Germany's reunification, not the end of World War II. Germany is both strong and weak, creator and victim of its own destiny. It is manipulated by fear more than anything else. Twenty years on, here we are.

XI
Four Possibilities

While writing this book, naturally, I studied the map of the eurozone—a map that European leaders say is ever more reminiscent of a battlefield. On this map, a single currency contends with overly large differential spreads on bonds issued in the same currency. In light of this, there are four possibilities for the future. We can:

– Passively allow a European Union catastrophe to unfold;

– Split the eurozone into stronger and weaker regions;

– Constitutionally reorganize the European Union, introducing greater budget discipline; making the European Central Bank a truly central bank; issuing Eurobonds and so forth;

– Find the courage to fight back and institute a New Alliance between people and states along the lines of Roosevelt's New Deal, which helped bring about the end of the Great Depression.

In part, the choice of one of those paths will simply rely on fate. But we have a say in things, too. If we choose together, we can determine our own fate.

As of this writing, the situation in Europe—no exaggeration here—recalls that of August 1914, when no single government act was decisive in determining the scope of the Great War, but at the same time no single government act was strong enough to stop it.

A series of causal and casual acts combined to lead to war. And there was something else happening, too. In the Thirty Years' War, the equilibrium of a peaceful world was disturbed by the Spanish ambassadors' desire for world domination. In 1914, it was the will of the powerful German state that threw things out of balance. Today, the combination of a greedy financial sector and the obtuse and weak sphere of politics is poised to be the decisive element. Meanwhile, the imbalances that the euro was supposed to address are emerging instead as a root cause of all of this. Indeed, those imbalances have stayed the same or, in some cases, worsened as a result of the crisis. We may still avoid a war in Europe, or a real war, at least.[18] No one in Europe seems inclined to jump into that circle of fire anymore. But if the fatal course of things is not interrupted, it is not implausible and would not be wholly unexpected for something to happen in Europe as it did during those earlier very dark times.

So, there are four possibilities. Their timing and impact varies, but all are possible, even probable, to varying degrees.

[18] Martin Feldstein, EMU and International Conflict, *Foreign Affairs* 1997, pp. 60–73.

Passively Await Catastrophe

The first possibility is the one most similar to the August 1914 scenario. It's the simplest, too, because it's automatic. It's also the most dramatic. It is the possibility of *continuity* leading *discontinuity*. In order for it to happen, we need only continue to do, or not do, what has been done, or not done, up until now. Just go along as we are and allow the greatest force at play to be the force imposed by events and their merciless sequential dictatorship: the force of inertia first, and then the force of gravity. The latter has us running, faster than ever before, across a sloping plain, toward a catastrophe that could recall the catastrophes of Europe's darkest hour.

There is no time to wait any longer. As we take our time, the clock is ticking. Whether we seek it or it is imposed on us, whether we are active or passive, whether we are conscious or unconscious, whether it is total or partial, our destiny awaits. It is leading us down this path, and that path has formed us culturally and spiritually during certain periods in history. I'm talking about the concept of *finis Europae*, as a result of decadence and suicidal urges. Do you smell a whiff of autumn breeze, of death, of Nietzschean-Dostoevskian thanatopolitics, a politics of death? Think of Dürer's famous woodcut of the four horsemen of the apocalypse, representing war, death, plague and famine. Famine is the most economics-related of the horsemen, and therefore the most relevant today. If this scenario comes true, we'll find ourselves in chaos, and we'll have to struggle to survive in a completely new reality. A reality in which there are no salaries and pensions, in which banks and ATM machines are shut down, in which hospitals can no longer provide medicine for patients. Schools will empty, while the squares and streets fill with rage. Historically, the end of a currency always has dramatic economic effects and tragic social effects.

Divide the Eurozone

We now come to the second possibility, dividing Europe into regions. This division could take one of two forms: one "soft" and one "hard," so to speak.

a) Let's begin with the "soft" form. The adverse conditions of the market and the difficulties some states are facing in placing their bonds on the market are encouraging more frequent appeals to the International Monetary Fund. Additionally, states that are having problems will likely eventually begin asking other states that are in better condition for assistance. Those states will then be in the best possible position in terms of their own interests and financial security in the eurozone. Note here that, given the conditions normally imposed by the International Monetary Fund (IMF), when a state goes to the IMF to seek aid , the state more or less cedes a certain amount of its national sovereignty. In other words, its hands are tied. Under this system, currency would remain the same formally, but a great political divide would open up within the eurozone. A gap would loom between states that retain their (dominant) national sovereignty and states that lose their sovereignty, by transferring it to the IMF. The latter states would become largely subordinate, outside of Europe while still a part of it. The loss of status on the part of states that are forced to go to the IMF can be dramatic and can itself cause division. Historically, IMF intervention has been imposed by technocrats who aren't capable of analyzing specific cases. Such intervention can last a long time and rarely is a happy experience for the countries involved. This rift between A-team states and B-team states in the eurozone would be the same. Ultimately, this kind of division would be even more marked and dramatic than the kind wrought by a formal division of the euro. Some states will enjoy full sovereignty and will be equipped with a strengthened currency; other states will lose sovereignty and will still suffer all the negative effects and limitations of the euro, without any of its benefits. The euro itself would survive, but as states were downgraded to B-team status, they would actually be paying for a so-called security measure that would benefit the other states.

b) The "hard" possibility is the breakup of the euro. The euro as we have known it until now may simply cease to exist, which would probably have very negative effects, first on the European economy, then on European politics and ultimately on the feelings that Europeans harbor about each other. The euro was created to achieve political union. If the euro were broken up, it would have the opposite effect. Again, the breakup of the euro would have not only monetary and economic repercussions, but perhaps most importantly, political repercussions as well. People do ask themselves these distressing questions about the fate of the euro, but they do so quietly. The questions arise in personal and bilateral meetings, in the offices and corridors of Brussels and in other capital cities. Now the financial market is posing this question, and it really wants an answer.

Rumor has it that some chancelleries are already drawing up a plan B. They're not looking for the end of the euro, but on the contrary are developing a defensive strategy to save the euro based on a new economically strengthened, if geographically limited, solidarity. The underlying corollary is that states that do not work based on these principles will be led to the exit.

Of course, that's just a rumor. Still, given the intensity of the crisis, it would be absurd to imagine that such a thing *isn't* being considered seriously. It is both welcomed and feared. On the one hand, the euro would be saved, but on the other, there is the survival of each individual country to consider.

This is an area where psychology and politics overlap: At the heart of plan B, fashioned as a new geopolitical general plan, stands a firmly held belief that currency is politically important. The idea is that a currency and its people share the same essence. A currency represents the nature of the people and vice versa.

This fetishistic and fundamentalist idea is ancient. Today, however, it contends with a new economic marketism, as well as new ways of thinking about power. It is an idea that may save us as easily as it may kill us. It grows out of a fear of disorder, of instability, of falling into chaos. Especially in Northern Europe, this idea is fuelled by the fear of having to pay for others, the fear of having to pour money that one has earned and saved into a bottomless pit, the fear of irregular monetary transfers. Behind all this stand the ghosts of the past and the demons of the present. Increasingly, German opinion polls show that:

1) People feel the postwar benefits of Europe have reached their peak; 2) public opinion, and therefore by extension the opinion of the new political class, is increasingly anti-European; 3) there is an increasing sense of the new postunification Germany's strength, role and global geopolitical positioning, and in relation to that, its old and oft-noted tendency toward military expansion is remaking itself in the form of equivalent expansion in the field of business; 4) the ghosts of the past and the fears of the present are growing and being revived. Technically, at the heart of plan B is the Kern-Euro plan, the euro of the nucleus, or the nucleus of the euro. This would be a form of monetary evolution suited to a weaker two-speed Europe. The plan calls for strict fiscal and monetary policy for a central nucleus, made up of Germany, the Netherlands, Austria, Luxembourg, Finland and potentially France, with a few new faces from the North and the East.

Almost all the other countries would remain outside the nucleus, forming the soft underbelly. This would lead to a double euro, one strong and one weak. A type of subeuro would be created and would be more commonly used as circulating currency and not as much for investment. Alternately, these states could return to their old national currencies, or perhaps create their own new currencies, with new names and symbols, in order to shield the eurozone from further damage. The understanding is that countries exiting the euro would place themselves under the tutelage of the IMF. This would be a new, updated version of the old two-speed Comecon that existed in Communist Eastern Europe, dominated by the Soviet Union. Or a new version of another, slightly older monetary order that was once imposed on Europe.

This is not the place to discuss in great depth the legal procedures that would be used in this more or less consensual operation, but it might involve something akin to the "reinforced cooperation" of the Schengen Agreement. The original Schengen Agreement protected against external political dangers, but this would be a new economic Schengen Agreement, designed to protect the center of Europe from external economic dangers.

Operating procedures would vary enormously depending on the timeframes and methods employed. There could be a technical split, with timings and methods mutually agreed upon, or there might be a big bang, created in a disorderly fashion by factors that bring the crisis to a head. In any case, such a scenario would doubtless be traumatic and dramatic.

Just imagine the procedures that would be required to reverse engineer the currency, going backward from the euro to the old national currencies and to other new national currencies with new names. There are simple logistical issues, like starting up the printing process for those national currencies again. Exchange rates would need to be set. Would we go back to 1999 rates, or attempt to create new ones from scratch? How to achieve the required balance of external and internal equality and the balance between public and private in each country? Could or should a choice be made to privilege one over the other, the internal over the external, the private over the public, or vice versa? In the end, but only after handling a series of serious and perhaps uncontrollable problems, could balance be achieved. History has shown this repeatedly.

There would probably be various advantages over the current situation. It's usually the debtors, such as states with their large public debts, that benefit from monetary upsets. Complex state budgets might benefit. A new national central bank could defend itself by doing something that the European Central Bank has so far failed to do—become the lender of last resort. A new currency, less alien and much closer to the true foundations of the economy, would encourage exports at its natural exchange rate, with no need to manipulate the rate. One could, after all, take the view that it might be a good thing to escape from the jaws of an overly strong currency that has proven more beneficial to the North than the South. That's true of the euro now, and it was true of the Italian lira a century and half ago.

But it would be better not to attempt this unless forced to do so, because the budget would also have to incorporate the risks of defaulting on public and private debt, the loss of capital, a drop in international confidence, fundamental in a globalized world, and as a result the possible shutdown of export channels. Above all, a process of this sort would require a long and serious recessionary period, and it would have serious, dramatic and unforeseeable political repercussions.

Things would also go very badly, indeed worse, in the so-called (self-defined) *Kern* or core of Europe: private and public loans to peripheral countries would have to be devalued or written off, causing huge damage; in the medium term, the economy would not remain competitive, but would most probably become less competitive than it is today. Exports, starting with cars, would be penalized not only by a higher and less favorable exchange rate, but by the hatred directed at those who caused and maybe even sought this chaos in Europe. After all, the majority of German exports still go to Europe. Ultimately, a kind of Germanophobia would take hold.

This would all end in capital draining way, and crises and disorders much worse than those currently expected in the areas of Europe that are deemed weak. The more things change, the more they stay the same, as the saying goes. Should one great country or a group of great countries hide away from it all in a tub like Diogenes?

Implement Constitutional Reorganization of Europe

The third possibility is the one that this book most favors, on the condition that it be politically integrated with the fourth possibility. I'm talking about a constitutional reorganization of Europe. This is the most difficult but also the most appealing route, if you consider that today in Europe there is a Union without union. Instead, division is the dominant force. Divisions at the lower levels, between debtor populations and creditor populations. Divisions at the higher levels, between the states in charge and the states that must obey them. Divisions, ultimately, between politicians who are beginning to think for themselves and politicians who still think on behalf of finance. Perhaps we bit off more than we could chew, and now it's time to take sensible bites. Something has to change, or we'll lose everything. In order to do this, however, we need to take a step backward and correct the original flaw. This flaw was not technical, but political: the flaw of considering the economy more important than politics. It was a mistake to think that the economy was a more accurate reflection of the lives, feelings and hearts of the people.

During the drama of German reunification, the natural

and historical law underlying Europe was inverted in order to avert a global crisis. That law states that economic unity comes first, followed by monetary unity. One cannot exist without the other. This was the so-called *Krönungstheorie*, the theory of coronation or culmination. It's no accident that all currencies incorporate and reflect the symbols of their civilizations and cultures, the lives and politics of their people. Currency is a reflection; it symbolizes something outside of itself. In any case, currencies have never done the work of politics. They can devastate politics, it is true. But they can't take political action. Those who used the euro to create Europe, to wind that crank and start the engine, exploited a real political need to do so. It wouldn't have been a good idea to unify Germany using the deutsche mark. Those who conjured up the formula for the euro made it seem like magic, like something they'd concocted during long hours in a laboratory, and they even got it right for a few years. But now they risk going down in history as having gotten it wrong.

Now everyone sees the euro not just as a means of saving the union, but also as a risky source of conflict. It's time to give people a voice once again. We need a reverse coronation to give the euro the political unity that it has never had and never managed to create.

If the original flaw was technical, rooted in the creation of the euro, and consequently the creation of the European Central Bank, the solution must and can only be political. This presents us with a large and very real dilemma: If we don't want to give up the common currency, it is clear that the crisis can only be subdued by introducing a different sort of shared management of that currency, beginning with expanding the role of the European Central Bank and Eurobonds. That, in turn, is only possible if a *new political agreement* can be created by and for all of Europe. If such an agreement were announced today with real determination and real efficiency, it might just suffice. It did suffice once, in May 2010. I won't go into the technical and judicial forms that this pact could take: a new treaty; a detailed interpretation of the European Union treaty, perhaps based on derivative regulation; a new intergovernmental agreement; reinforced cooperation. Just one fundamental caveat must be imposed, given that the devil is in the details: If Europe is constitutionally reorganized only partially, with fiscal discipline, but without a new European Central Bank or Eurobonds, as was floated at the summit of December 8 to 9, 2011, or, worse still, if it is agreed that it will be reorganized only if certain countries are preemptively assigned parking spaces in the IMF garage, then this third possibility will end up being too similar to the second possibility. As such, it will be unacceptable, as it would be too divisive.

What is therefore now very important is that, in order for true constitutional reorganization to take place and Europe as we know it to be saved, a real political trade-off is needed. This would involve both greater budget discipline, based on a shared governance, with commitments, controls and sanctions, and a better integrated and more mutual management of currency, with state bonds in the form of Eurobonds. But we need both, not the first without the second, nor the second without the first.

Great political skill encompassing historical vision and intelligence would be needed to enact this scenario. Historical vision would be particularly important to ending the era of deficit spending. The problems of public finance that still exist in various countries are problems rooted in the past. They are serious problems and need to be dealt with as problems of the past and not ongoing problems in the present that will continue into the future. Intelligence is needed to understand that, while some countries may react poorly to suggestions that their economic structures and public finances need correcting, other countries have made very effective progress after finding themselves in difficulty by acting with an eye to social and democratic cohesion.

It is still not clear what will happen. Possibly under the dramatic pressure of the crisis change will be enlightened and sudden and will in the end take the form of a shock to the political system. Unfortunately, it seems more likely to follow a longer and more tortuous route, as the December 2011 summit suggests. This process runs the risk of a market crash. After all, the financial market operates day in and day out and employs a type of simple and unsophisticated binary intelligence that responds to simple stimuli: yes or no, black or white, no gray areas allowed.

Create a New Alliance

The fourth and last possibility is that of resistance, an alliance between people and states, a courageous path that leads to an exit strategy.

Today the risk is higher than ever that the saying "anything is possible" will turn out to be true. The last European summit, which major players claim should have been the last summit ever, was held in Brussels December 8 to 9, 2011. European heads of state and government attended. The resulting fiscal compact was instantly, and perhaps unfairly, termed the "fiasco compact" by English-language financial websites. That old May spirit had been tamped down, and it wasn't so easy to bring it back. The idea that France pushed for the introduction of the "golden rule" of a balanced budget isn't exactly credible, given that France itself was so far from achieving that. The numerous and various divisive statements made after the event were the straw that broke the camel's back.

The most striking thing that emerged was the image of Europe that was created by this new, hypothetical, severe policy of a strict and binding approach to public budgets. That image is essentially financial and punitive. There is a risk that the new strictness will do little to pull public debt out of the fire, and instead will result in symmetrical, simultaneous parallel deflation and depression in the real European economy. That would aggravate the crisis rather than resolving it. Starting with the collapse in the value of assets and portfolios, it would not attract capital but rather encourage capital flight.

The summit was similar to the third scenario, in which the European Union is constitutionally reorganized, but with a fundamental limitation: The mechanism of strictness and rigor to create fiscal union is imposed, but the mechanism of solidarity is missing. This is serious, because the most critical structural issue within the European Union would be overlooked and therefore left untouched. Even if fiscal union were achieved at the upper level, as proposed at the last summit, too many large differences would persist between the real economies underlying it. What has been forgotten, in particular, is that real differences, which exist now and would continue to exist, cannot be bridged simply by reinforcing the internal market or even by increasing the number of European regulations. Doing so requires implementing the decisive force of Eurobonds to make developmental and unifying public investments.

So, all of these possibilities are possible, obviously, but how probable are they? That's difficult to predict at this time. Purely as a guideline, without committing completely, we can theorize as follows:

a) The first possibility is now not only possible, but probable. If it does play out, it will be a tragedy.

b) The second possibility is not only still possible, but it has also become more probable. What makes it unlikely for now, however, is still the problem of how to implement it. Because, unlike the first scenario, which would happen automatically, this one requires a certain amount of political will. So far nobody has admitted to having the will to see it through. Indeed, the leaders have announced that they intend to attempt to implement the third possibility, constitutional reorganization.

c) The third possibility is still possible, and its probability depends on us. It depends on the political determination that we, peoples and states, want to invest in the constitutional reorganization of Europe. As noted above, this is the preferred possibility. Preferred, however, only on the condition that it is complete and politically integrated with the fourth possibility, below. A possibility based not only on fiscal union, but based also on Eurobonds, so that Europe is more than just a financial prison. It is for this reason that the December 2011 summit doesn't seem to have resolved anything: It simultaneously went too far and not far enough. It was too strict on public budgets, and it wasn't strict enough in other areas, namely Eurobonds. In any case, timing is key. The possibility of a crash looms over the entire process, because political time isn't on the same schedule as financial time and thought and action still don't seem convincingly connected.

d) The fourth possibility is to employ an exit strategy, as set out in the following pages.

Whichever scenario becomes reality, a negative one such as the first or second, or a positive one such as the third, it is still useful to look into the near future.

XII
The New Alliance

This crisis marks a turning point in history. Once it was a prediction, today it is a fact.[19] Not only has our economic and social system ground to a halt, but in suddenly shifting from a national scale to a global one, passing from an old type of capitalism to a new one, from a solid state to a liquid one, it has dramatically ceased to be what it once was—a system.

What we are witnessing and experiencing today is not just a phase but a paradigm shift. Like the difference in viewpoint between Ptolemy and Copernicus: The sun doesn't rise anymore. The earth's horizon sinks. To be clear, the sun that doesn't rise anymore is automatic and guaranteed development and wellbeing, made freely possible by the magic of finance. Yet through its magicians, followers and disciples, all permanently in its employ, it wreaks disaster.

We can no longer live in debt. To do so would risk redistributing the little wealth that we still produce

[19] See G. Tremonti, *The Hope and the Fear.*

toward the top. We are eroding, or we risk eroding the foundation of our civilized life, of our democracy and, ultimately, of our morals. That is precisely where this technical *ruptus* will lead. Not reducing the cost of finance, but recalculating the perimeters of life, weighing medical care in terms of the hole it creates in the public budget, bringing potential life expectancy—and, of course, living is much more costly when you are old or ill or both—in line with a balanced budget. Benevolent consolation is offered to those who will live shorter lives—after all, it's the quality of life that counts, not the quantity of years, or so a "healthy society" tells us.

When civilizations are in crisis, fascism and its cousins immediately show up on the scene and volunteer to help it progress. They move easily between different areas, too, from finance to social engineering. We cannot afford to ignore reality—it has been said, and it must be repeated that in the West we can no longer live in debt—but instead must adapt to the current reality in the best and most humane way possible. The best possible way to do this is using political methods, not technical ones. The solution must be political, not apolitical.

This is as ambitious and as difficult as it is necessary. We shouldn't try to manage a reality that cannot be managed, because that would generate a chain reaction of crises. Instead, we should begin writing a new social contract.

We know exactly what we shouldn't do: continue on as if nothing's wrong, as if a financial recovery could take place within the current system. Simply taking a just and effective approach is good, but it's still not enough.

If it were enough, we could simply implement the largest bankruptcy settlement ever and leave just a few standing on the field. We could implement a relentless sequence of financial maneuvers that, one after the other, would be used up and discarded. We could take a slash and burn approach. But that would lead to social unrest. Entire countries would be stripped bare. It would be like committing suicide just for the purpose of declaring bankruptcy.

Carefully thought out and well-balanced steps toward financial recovery are necessary, but they are not and will never be sufficient on their own. That's due to the internal workings of this so-called system. If the effort is limited to subduing it and still not aimed at changing it, or abandoning it, it will never work.

We must all give some thought to the matter. We mustn't think in a passive, fatalistic or conventional way. We mustn't be slaves to or victims of the tyranny of reality and its absurd current financial status quo. Instead, we must imagine that a different reality is possible. As I will seek to demonstrate here, while it's true that there is much to avoid, there isn't really all that much that needs to be invented. The best thing to do is not to blaze an entirely new path, but to follow a path that already exists, although it's hidden in our recent past. We were lured off of that path, first by fervent belief in the financial market and then by a kind of collective madness, and we tried to bury it, to hide it, to erase it from our social map.

History never repeats itself exactly, right down to the last detail. But there is both a possible and probable analogous solution to what we're experiencing and witnessing today, above all in Europe, in the midst of an economic and political crisis. In this analogous episode, old systems were replaced by a new one, and consequently the United States was able to end the Great Depression of 1933, using the principles of the New Deal. Today the time has come for a New Alliance in Europe, between people and nations.

It won't be easy, but we need to begin to shape and build this alliance, person by person, community by community. We need to develop it in workplaces and schools, in think tanks and political institutions. We must implement it, country by country, tracing the pattern of a political and moral design, sewing the stars onto a new flag, similar to the one that flew proudly for decades throughout the West.

What we need now is both community thinking and social thinking. As a way of setting out some concrete parameters, I am listing a few simple working ideas for politics and policy:

1) There is no politics without feelings, and the feelings characteristic of a politics worthy of this name are only moral feelings. It should always be this way, but it is above all in moments of crisis that the value of moral

feelings rises to the fore. Politics is not and cannot be an end (in itself); it is a means. A means to do something, something possible, right and just. Today we are living at the end of a world that for a while, more or less twenty years, has drugged and deluded us with the notion that finance was freely giving us ongoing well-being. In this world, the impossible and the unthinkable became possible and real, and excess mattered more than necessities. This incredibly potent drug has not completely wiped away the past. Many of us, especially in the older generations, remember with difficulty, but we do remember. Most of today's young people have known only this world in their lifetimes. That's why the end of this world is alienating, annihilating and hitting them hardest of all. (I'll come back to young people later.) The return to reality is hard for everyone, but it's hardest for young people. They see the end of a society where desires are satisfied for free. The return to a world in which trees don't grow top down, but rise from the ground; a world in which the instruments of work matter more than financial instruments, in which tools matter more than futures contracts.

We're headed back to the past whether we do it on purpose or not due to a slowdown in the global economy. Regaining a sense of limits and discipline, of duty and sacrifice. Restoring value and dignity to all of these ancient words.

There is no totalitarian machine that can reconstruct the world. No ideology can make that promise or claim.

But we must and we can have faith, whether religious or secular. For those who do believe, we need faith in the ability to turn the city of man into the city of God. Faith, whatever your beliefs, in our ability progressively and cooperatively to adapt reality to our ideals.

Not through individual actions taken by individuals, but through joint acts, inspired by shared plans. In particular, this cannot be achieved through individual, though laudable, donations. All of this must be done as part of a broad and organic plan that encompasses, develops and promotes the idea of the common good, and so once again focuses on family, community and the state.

2) What is certain—and to be certain of this you need only read the next chapter—is that a politics of this type is neither right-wing nor left-wing, because it is no longer definable along the lines of old ideological categories.

Nor is it an anti-market politics, at least not in the original *Wealth of Nations* notion of the market: wealth, yes, but nations, too, and not a degeneration of the market into marketism.

The financial market can impose a state of emergency and act as a nondemocratic political superpower to defend its interests, and as long as it invokes the state we're not shocked. So we shouldn't be surprised either when it urges a return to market regulation "wherever possible," and only in the communities and states "where necessary." We especially shouldn't be surprised if all of this is organized in the political form preferred here, the social economy of the market. In *The Fear and the Hope,* I predicted "the clamorous return of the public hand." The public hand then effectively returned and it has been used, but unfortunately it has mostly been used poorly, to save finance. Here is one last chance to use it again, but better.

3) Certainly a politics of this type will only work if it is backed by conviction and courage; courage because in wishing to reestablish politics over the economy, the just in place of the unjust, law in place of abuse, the notion of common good in place of the myth of individual enterprise, this politics not only goes against a highly powerful block of established interests, but also tries to dismantle them, reconstructing the traditional hierarchy of civic values. This type of politics has its own strengths, however: It is not a politics that works in the interests of the few, but one that works in the interests of the many; it is a politics that does not breathe with the troubled and tragic trembling panting of the last ephemeral twenty years, but takes the deep and even breaths of history.

4) This type of politics must be concrete, from the Latin *cum crescere*, grow together. For this reason, it cannot be made up of top-down ideas, of cold, remote and technocratic ideas. Indeed, those signaled the end of the European ideal. It wasn't like this at the start. At the start, the message was strong, warm and capable of capturing the

hearts and minds of the people. Great leaders spoke of peace between peoples, of carbon and steel, energy and agriculture. Now we hear only the cold numeric facts of the spread differentials on bonds—bonds that are paradoxically denominated in a currency that should be the common currency.

This politics must be not only concrete, but credible. At the moment, through no fault of its own, politics has become barely credible and focused on a false objective. And this has put it under stress from two directions: On the one hand, politics can no longer do what it did before, because the crisis has radically reduced its traditional means of intervention (public expenditure and fiscal reduction), and on the other hand, the people who are under pressure from the crisis due to inertia—after all, this is the way things have been done for decades—continue to demand more of politics. Rather than telling them the truth, politics continues to dupe them.

If many people are turning toward a false objective or applying themselves to achieving it, no one, or very few people at least, is pointing fingers at the true culprit, finance.

Politics can move on from this stalemate, from this phase of culpable collusion and lack of willpower and again put itself at the service of the people, only if it has the strength to create a concrete and decisive mood, the strength to place itself above finance. The strength to present itself not as the cause of problems, but as their possible solution. Just as in the past, states, politics and governments can and therefore must take up their scepters, in the name of the people and for the public good.

5) Our societies are old, so they need shock treatment. Not in the form of a traumatic shock, such as a war or revolution (although honestly the latter cannot be ruled out). But a political shock. Such as? There is only one option: Change the constitutions to give young people twice the voting power of everyone else. That way, young people, who are a minority, can determine the future. They're the ones who will be around in the future, so they're highly invested in it, but they're underrepresented demographically. At the turn of the 19th century universal suffrage won out over census suffrage, which favored the rich and the elite. Now youth suffrage can create an equal, if different and new form of social justice.

6) A politics of this nature must be democratic, however. If it is not democratic, in the sense of truly being based on popular consensus, then it does not exist. It is not hard for it to be this way. When things are going well, politics tends to promise riches for everyone. When things aren't going well, politics must instead guarantee security. In times of crisis, it cannot and does not posit or promise impossible heaven on earth scenarios. Obviously, it can't even come close to offering that during and after a crisis. But it can and must instead guarantee the most important thing: security.

7) Given the legal, economic and social interconnections that are in place in Europe, a politics of this nature cannot be deployed in a single member state. It must be as widespread as possible in Europe. It cannot stop at old national boundaries. Essentially, it is based on the idea that it can and must overcome the old boundaries by flying over them.

It can't be limited to the statement issued by Germany's Constitutional Court not too long ago, which claimed that Europe has a democracy deficit because it lacks the *demos,* or a uniform European people. In the United States, too, there is no "uniform people," as the Germans put it, but instead a heterogeneous population made up of people of different geopolitical origins, races, cultures, religions, practices and customs, and you would be hard-pressed to prove that democracy is lacking in the United States.

8) This is not, perhaps, the moment to discuss the future political organization likely to take shape after the final positive or negative discussions of the euro.

Of course, if a common Europe is sought under certain political conditions, one must also accept, as an alternative to economic dictatorship or the dictatorship of financial technocracy, a greater degree of common democratic policy. That must begin with the largest powers in the European Parliament, and it must lead to bringing back the European regions from the depths of history. On the other hand, technical institutions such as the European Central Bank must take appropriate steps backward. Rather than advancing across the field shamefully abandoned by politics, they should return to or remain in their predetermined and limited technical fields of action. That will reestablish the natural boundaries of democratic political sovereignty.

9) The political difficulties and challenges that we are now facing can be overcome using the Internet, the most suitable platform for this new type of politics.

We can come together on the Internet not only in order to count each other, but also simply to count, to matter. We as a group have the power and duty to act if we want to see the return of useful politics.

Politics can advance if it returns to its once noble heights. But it can do so only if it has the ability to recover the good from the past. This includes the ability to fuse the particular with the general and the internal with the external. It means regaining the ability to have and to represent a general vision inspired by common interests, and the ability to take care of one's own business. These ideals and values cross over national boundaries—they actually overcome these boundaries. These are ideas that can grow and flourish without damaging the roots of their neighbors or the weak. The ideals most suited to uniting us in common spirit are general and moral ideals and therefore by definition they are not selfish. These are community ideals, social ideals.

There are, as we shall see, at least three places where

such ideals should be implemented. Doing this means putting ourselves on the right path, the path toward planning an exit strategy.

There is a certain type of politician of whom it is said, he knows how to govern but not how to get reelected. This is how people are tricked and politicians come to be replaced by technocrats who do not need, or do not believe that they need, the people. The time has come to break this cycle.

The logic, the political essence inherent to the pattern traced in this book brings peoples and states closer together. It moves them toward a New Alliance. There, fears and protests and the needs and fundamental rights of the people can work in conjunction with the states' repossession of power.

The situation is not only very difficult, but it is also very different from country to country, different because of discrepancies between their situations and the issues they face, because of ratios of public to private debt, but it is imperative that we make a virtue of necessity. We must yank out the cause of the crisis, the excessive power of finance, at its roots. It is imperative that we return to regulation and create plans for great public investments for the common good at the heart of the economy. It is essential that we rebalance the positions of creditors and debtors, avoiding the kind of overcorrection that can lead to a depression, and preserving the industrial and economic bases of individual countries. Those will be essential to financing the recovery. In order to do this, it is fundamental that we return to using words and phrases such as regulation, hope and dignity, common good, family, community and state. All this is necessary, no matter how difficult it may be.

XIII
The Exit Strategy

We can no longer confuse the illness with the medicine and thus continue to have faith in finance and its prescriptions. It is not wise to sit and wait for economic growth to accelerate miraculously. Indeed, as noted earlier, it would be wiser to equip ourselves differently. We need to value the ethical and moral considerations of equality and justice that are becoming more and more relevant precisely because of the crisis.

It is hard to believe that inflation will save us, especially when the European Central Bank and China fear it so. Of course, as a large creditor, China has a lot to lose, as the value of the payments due to it would sink, and it would therefore become socially destabilized.

It is not sensible to wait for a war to liberate us. Wars are, admittedly, monstrous accelerators of the economy. When Germany entered World War II, it was still using horses, and it came out of it using V2 tanks. Yet only "great" wars produce this crazy accelerating effect. They have to be wars between great powers for the economy to feel a positive effect. They can't be wars of great powers against nonexistent or imagined powers. The accelerating effect that wars produce occurs only in relation to world wars, not local ones, actual tragedies and not simply acts of economic opportunism. No, thanks.

This is why the exit strategy can only be realized through great politics, in a New Alliance between peoples and states. Putting the state above finance and finance below the state; making regulation prevail over anarchy; launching large public works projects for the common good. It can and it must begin with an individual state, but then it is essential that it spread to others. Let us attempt, then, to imagine the beginnings of our different future, as set out below:

– Reject the laws in force and return to the letter and the spirit of the old glorious banking laws modeled on the Glass-Steagall Law of 1933, written to separate the productive economy from the speculative economy.

– Push forward and adopt, in the form of a new multilateral international treaty, the OECD rules on the principles of pertinence, transparency and integrity in the economy.

– Introduce Eurobonds.

We should consider the possibility of taxing financial transactions with something like the Tobin tax. This should be approached with a certain degree of caution, but it should not be flat out rejected. We must consider this cautiously for two reasons: This type of taxation has already been shot down in the main non-European financial centers, such as the City, Wall Street and the

Asian centers, so its unpopularity in those places could harm Europe. Also, ironically, if introduced, this type of tax would legalize—after the fact—the very financial transactions that should have been strongly prohibited before the crisis.

Putting the State Above Finance and Finance Below the State

Two centuries ago, in 1816, Thomas Jefferson wrote, "I sincerely believe . . . that banking establishments are more dangerous than standing armies." Today, the situation is more or less the same, and that is why the time has come to put the state above finance, and finance below the state. The time has come to impose limits on finance's excessive power. To do this would put an end once and for all to two decades that saw private interests unnaturally valued over public ones. It would "drive the merchants from the Temple," breaking the spell of power still wielded by the money gurus.

Doing this would mean that only the state would issue money in the name of the people. It would mean that credit would be used for development and not speculation. It would mean separating the wheat from the chaff, the productive from the speculative, as was done for centuries. It would mean beginning to defend and stabilize public budgets. All in all it would pave the way for a different economic and social system. That system would not only be more ethical, but would also be more effective than the monetary system that is now crumbling and is unfortunately dragging us down with it. And we're going down if we don't resist, if we don't react, if we don't change.

I must repeat that the time has come to redistribute power between finance and the states. We need to bring balance back to the relationship between finance, which developed for its own interests, and politics, tasked with representing the general interests of the community. Even in the worst possible political scenario of a politics of truly debatable value, there is still debate, and a debatable politics is still better than an unquestionable financial system. Winston Churchill once said, "Democracy is the worst form of government except all the others." Financial autocracy can't possibly be better than democracy.

The financial and banking world that we face today is very diversified, both nationally and on a European level. And that's not all. There is no single intervention to plan, no single tool that can be used to fix things. There is, however, a common political logic that can be placed at the heart of every intervention. In some cases, this means making the banks—which still are and/or still say they are systemic—less systemic, non-systemic. This means reducing their size, dividing them into parts, stripping them of powers. The time has come to separate production from speculation. The time has come to separate banks that gather savings and capital and invest them, at their own risk, in great industries, in small businesses, for families, for communities and for young people from banks that gamble, privatizing their gains and socializing their losses. This separation would produce the opposite of today's capitalistic efficiency. The banks must therefore once again be treated like infrastructures that serve the economy and society, not the other way around. In some cases the banks will have to be nationalized perhaps at the expense of the community. Better to act in advance, before they are in so much trouble that it becomes urgent.

The wheat must be separated from the chaff, the good from the bad. Accounting books will have to be reopened, possibly by force. Voluntary and compulsory investigations will be have to be carried out to determine how much wheat and chaff is contained in each bank, before investigations move on to every big financial operator.[20]

The healthy ones will have to be distinguished from the toxic ones, which will be quarantined. Various ancient and modern techniques can be applied to implement this quarantine. Those range from sabbaticals to moratoria to categorization as bad banks. But it is clear that the huge toxic financial mass, which is still operating within the current system, must be phased out as gradually as possible and unloaded onto speculators or written off. Gamblers cannot be allowed simply to walk

[20] The author envisioned a similar scenario as early as 2007. (See Appendices 3 and 12.)

away from the gambling table and let others absorb their losses. Those who have gambled and lost must be held to account for those losses.

We have got to get the virus that started in finance and is propagating itself everywhere it goes under control.

Many banking and financial parties, businesses and groups must be nudged toward orderly bankruptcy proceedings. Those proceedings could be modeled on Chapter 11 bankruptcy in the United States. We cannot pretend we will be able to save everything, especially when experience teaches us that in trying to save everything, we inevitably end up saving the worst parts.

At the time of the New Deal, beginning in 1933, first new rules were introduced and the banking and financial system was reorganized, cutting off its parasitic activity. Then public money was used for public investments, for infrastructure, and to support families and industries. (More on this type of investment below.) Incidentally, it should be pointed out here that if the American industrial system hadn't been saved, the Americans wouldn't have been able to help fight the Nazis.

In 2008, the opposite was done: Public money was mostly used to save banks and bankers; new rules were not created (quite the opposite); no serious large-scale public investment projects in the industrial, physical and manufacturing economy, or in infrastructure, were announced.

What should now be done wholeheartedly and as a priority is instead to focus first on surviving. We should abandon the model of the so-called universal bank, which is the DNA of the systemic bank, the basis of the bankrupt global megabanks. To do this a new, updated version of the Glass-Steagall Act of 1933 should be introduced.[21]

In short, now as in the past, we need to build a firewall between ordinary banks and risky banks, so that the ordinary banks can no longer lend their current account holders' money to risky banks, or buy their structured products. A distinction must and can be made instantaneously. We should discard the new laws, most of which were introduced in the 1990s, and return to the old laws of the 1930s. This is what should be done. We can't just create firewalls within the old banks as if nothing happened.

It is true that enormous profits can be made by speculating with money deposited in banks by ordinary account holders. But this is precisely what needs to be stopped. Account holders' money and taxpayers' money should no longer be exposed to this kind of risk, a kind of risk that is now spreading to public budgets and, as the scale of the crisis grows, is affecting everyday people's well-being and lives, too.

This is not all that needs to be done. It will also be necessary to reduce the risk from derivatives. We can apply the same technique here: Discard the laws that since the 1990s have given derivatives free reign in the United States and Europe.

[21] For further information on the Glass-Steagall Act, see Appendix 13.

In any case, it is essential that ordinary banks not be allowed to negotiate and/or acquire derivatives in any form.

This must be done so that banks continue to be banks, doing only what they can and must do, in service to the economy and to society, to great industries and small businesses, to communities, families and young people. To reduce the addiction to the drug of profit at any cost, a ban should be introduced on booking the profits of what are called upfronts on the basis of the net present value principle. This calculation method is based on counting in advance profits that are expected to be derived in the future from a financial operation carried out today. It wildly increases the risk level of financial operations. Probably not coincidentally, it also increases bonuses. If a new sane accounting principle is not introduced—a principle that permits gains to be recorded only after they have actually been made and not just when they are expected to be made in the future—then moral hazard will continue to be rewarded. Everyone will continue to pursue reckless financial operations, because they'll have a chance to turn a profit by gambling on the future, and there will be no certainty that the lender of last resort will intervene in the case of a loss. The ban on derivatives starting with credit default swaps and limits on rating agencies are discussed above. All of this is not an exaggeration. It's difficult. But it's simple, too, in the sense that it simply must be done.

Making Rules Prevail Over Anarchy

Speaking of the current semianarchy, an important minister stated, "With regard to Bretton Woods, there are in reality, juridical differences. Bretton Woods took the form of a treaty which would be ratified by the various parliaments. We didn't want this kind of complication." But this is exactly what is needed! To quote Saint Augustine: "If you take away law, what is there to distinguish the state from a band of brigands?" Positivist contemporary thought says that law is not based on a natural state of "being" but on "what one should be." Today we find ourselves in a legal paradox. That paradox has created a vacuum, and in that vacuum, finance functions on the principle that there is no "being" or sense of self in regulations, nor is there any sense of how things should be underlying them. Without rules, any attempt to overcome the crisis will only set the stage for a new one. Not to mention that, should this crisis continue, as it might, justice will be required. Justice can only be created by new rules, and then those new rules could be employed to offset any new injustices that would be caused by this continuation of the crisis.

To create a different future, we need new rules. Among those who won't agree with this are the disciples and promoters of the theory of economic naturalism, who are ideologically opposed to any "artificial" normative intervention in the market. They consider the market a "natural" and therefore neutral and apolitical place.

In reality, the market does not exist only in nature; it is a place at once natural and artificial. The spirit moves the market, but it is also constructed and organized on the basis of political decisions. These are the invisible hands of the law and of regulations, and they keep the flesh from succumbing completely to the spirit.

Laws and regulations. Not auto-regulation or self-regulation. The prefixes *auto-* and *self-* cancel any meaning in the words law and regulation.

Indeed, self-regulation is typical of peripheral areas of society and the economy. It is more recently typical of finance and usually follows a corporate logic.

Self-regulation can therefore play a complementary role, but not a fundamental or established role. The experience of the Financial Stability Board proves this beyond any doubt.

A strategy for exiting from a broken down system and anarchy requires something different from the norm, something stronger. At the present time, in the global market, under the pressure of the crisis, we have come up with the idea of the Global Legal Standard (GLS). Kant's *jus cosmopoliticum*, a truly global political system, may be an old idea, but it is an idea that is perfectly suited to our times.

If the 20th century was the century of the gold exchange standard, this century can and must be identified by a new, different, legal global parameter: the Global Legal Standard, which I proposed at a seminar in Paris in 2008, and then again in Italy at the G7 in 2009.

The approach is outlined in this set of rules, approved by the OECD:

1) Accuracy, integrity and transparency are the cornerstones of an economy that requires the support and the confidence of the public and that responds to the latter's demands and expectations.

2) Efficient competition is indispensable for an efficient and healthy market and reinforces productivity and economic growth. Anticompetition practices must be punished and discouraged, and useless restrictions placed on competition by public powers must be eliminated.

3) Corporate governance should promote respect for the primacy of the law and the responsibility of the Administrative Council as well as the fair treatment of and appropriate cooperation with interested parties. Remuneration and incentives should be in line with the long-term objectives of the companies and with risk policies.

4) Policies on the release of information about companies should be adapted to the nature, size and location of said companies; such policies should promote effective transparency and guarantee the dissemination of up-to-date and precise information regarding the assets, the financial standing, the nonfinancial results, and the respect of the company for principles of responsible investment, as well as the foreseeable risks (especially social, ethical and environmental risks), and details of the shareholders and the governance of those same companies.

5) Corporate structures should not be used for illicit

purposes. Corporate decisions should properly bear in mind the norms of responsible corporate conduct. The company's responsibilities include ensuring that it accurately satisfies the fiscal obligations of all the countries in which it is present at the time in question. Businesses must respect the letter and spirit of fiscal legislation.

6) Corruption, and more specifically corruption in international economic operations compromises good governance and sustainable economic development and alters the conditions of international competition. It would be appropriate to adopt efficient measures of prevention (through the use of awareness campaigns in particular), of penal procedure and of suppression.

7) The laundering of capital constitutes a serious threat to the world economy, compromises the integrity of financial institutions and should be legally prosecuted and punished.

8) The interaction between public powers and businesses (including, given that they concern public contracts, lobbying and so-called "revolving door" practices between a public office and the private sector) should base itself on the principles of transparency, integrity and equality with regard to all parties.

9) The regulatory organization of business and market activities should: pursue clearly identified strategic objectives and create advantages which justify their costs; respect the principles of necessity, feasibility and transparency; and be subjected to ongoing evaluation of their impact.

10) Effective financial regulation is essential in order to sustain the good working order and stability of the financial system. The financial education and protection of consumers constitutes an important element of such an organization. The responsibility and transparency of financial institutions and of financial brokerage should be encouraged until these same institutions provide fair and transparent information and advice to their clients, and promote their clients' financial awareness.[22]

Large Public Works for the Common Good

After the war, the car was the biggest and strongest driver of development. To begin with, it created economic development: metal, glass, a need to manufacture components, as well as cement and asphalt to create a place where those cars could circulate. Along with those came the promotion of a new lifestyle, inspired by the dream and then the reality of the car. A lifestyle that for decades shaped life around freedom and progress.

Today we do not have such a driver, a strong, visible and useful part of our lives that gives life a purpose. The new economy did not and does not perform that function. Despite its advancement, evolution and

[22] For further information on the process whereby this set of rules could be transformed into a multilateral international treaty, see Appendix 14.

importance, it has been and is merely instrumental: It is to development what energy or the electric light were to industry. They made it (and they still make it) work and operate well, but they were not and they are not, except in a very conventional sense, themselves industry.

This having been said, it should be noted that the modern economy is hovering between two general models: one liberal and monetary model and one mixed and varied model that to varying degrees can encompass the typical elements if not of the controlling economy, then of the social economy of the market and of public demand.

The first is a postmodern model, made up of two basic components: internal demand and export.

Following this model today is precarious for two reasons: because within a society that is wealthy, if not ostentatiously so, internal demand, predominantly for consumer goods, tends naturally to reach the saturation point; and because exports depend on choices, facts, external events and therefore have a high rate of uncontrollable variability.

Then there's the other model, which is created by adding another component to the first two: the component of public demand for public investment in the collective interest. Demand for vast and necessary programs of public investment aimed at the common good, beginning with infrastructure. These may take tangible and/or physical form as well as intangible form.

This model is obviously also based on the state, and

therefore it differentiates itself from the monetary model, which is based solely on the market. Incidentally, looking at the geoeconomic map of the world and using a metric that is not limited to the instantaneous ephemera of the short term, today it is clear that the first model isn't winning. It's not performing so well. The second model is more effective and can probably now prevail, after decades of monetarism and anti-industrial politics.

And it's what we need, on a large scale. Eurobonds are part of it, and they must not be purely financial instruments. Instead, they should be firmly grounded in industry.

The history of Eurobonds can be summarized as follows:

At the heart of the matter is the idea of a European Union bond, an idea put forward for the first time in 1993 by Jacques Delors, then president of the European Union. It was intended to finance European infrastructural investments and to do much more. The idea was to draw on the so-called Maastricht dividend to promote economic growth in Europe. The slogan was *Growth, Employment and Competitiveness*.

This idea languished in political desk drawers for ten long years. It was only taken up again in the second term of 2003, when Italy held the European presidency. At that time, citing the Delors plan as a starting point, I included Delors' idea in the official Italian program, and argued for it not just on economic grounds but above all on political ones: It is partly a financial technique, built on the original premise of financing large European infrastructures, including the defense industry and the green economy. But above all it is a political idea in the style of Hamilton, the first Secretary of the Treasury of the United States of America, who believed that with a little money, you could build a great nation.

Initial reaction was negative: bureaucratic, said the European Commission; impulsive, said Germany, still afflicted with the Weimar syndrome, the permanent fear of hyperinflation and thus automatically voting "no" on public debt, whether national or European; political, said the United Kingdom, because to the United Kingdom Eurobond = Eurobudget, and Eurobudget = European super state. No, thanks!

Since then, the notion of Eurobonds has only been discussed academically and in passing. It is only because of the crisis that it came roaring back onto the scene. Let's call it the Juncker-Tremonti Proposal (as the *Financial Times* did on December 5, 2010). Others followed. The 2010 proposal is a mere variation of the original idea of 1993, followed ten years later by that of 2003. It differs in its implementation: not gathering private capital on the markets to finance European public investments, but instead issuing European public bonds on the markets, with the aim of stabilizing and normalizing the issues. This would avoid any additional cost caused by speculation and lack of confidence in Europe on the part of the markets, because they no longer understand its purpose. The two ideas for Eurobonds, the first more industrial and the second more financial, are not at odds with either the spirit or the letter of the European Union treaties. If kept below 60% of public debt, and so under the ceiling imposed by the treaties, as the Juncker-Tremonti Proposal provides, Eurobonds would be perfectly compatible with the extant treaty and there would be no need to increase debt beyond currently consented levels. After all, in 2008, in the first phase of the crisis, the treaties were very flexibly interpreted when it came to introducing measures to handle the crisis. In any case, if the treaties needed to be modified for political reasons before Eurobonds could be issued, in order to ensure strong governance, that would be a good thing and not a bad thing, an investment, not an expense.

To sum up, the two Eurobond ideas, those of 1993 and 2003 and that of 2010, reflect and apply the same strong, sound political logic. This type of logic is all the more necessary if one considers that we are heading for a not insubstantial period of economic crisis. During that time it will be vital to control and reduce the cost of public debt, but also to increase public investments, under the just logic of a mixed economy. And yet that economy will not be based only on the (bankrupt) monetary and liberal methods or solely on the theory of the monopolistic state, but on a suitable combination of the two.

What should be avoided however is the recent sophistry against Eurobonds: Eurobonds presuppose a European fiscal union that stabilizes and normalizes public finances, but if the required stability is achieved, then

Eurobonds will no longer be necessary. That isn't true. The dilemma the European Union faces is more dramatic than that: Can it have fiscal union at the upper levels if at the lower levels there are fundamental structural differences in the real economy?

It is obvious that, in the area covered by the Union, there are still huge and real differences. Differences that stem from each country's history, geography, and demographics. It could be that this imbalance between fiscal union and real economy would be overcome by reinforcing the internal market. This process might be necessary, but it will never be sufficient on its own. It is for this reason, too, that Europe now needs public investment in new large developmental and interconnected infrastructures.

If bad politics generates corruption, bad finance generates something even worse: destruction. It cannot be said that a complete organized absence of politics leads to salvation, for the simple reason that the void left by politics has been and is filled by finance.

The alternative to these financial autocracies is twofold: a productive economy and governments that join together and actively commit to investment programs for the common good. Indeed, that is the objective purpose of governments. It's the very reason governments exist, whether national or European.

As stated, the plans detailed above, on the state-bank relationship, on the law-market relationship, on the private-public relationship, are only the first. They are not, as I have stated, completely new ideas: They reflect and contain the experiences of the past. They are updated versions. However, just as they were fundamental then, so they can and must be fundamental now. Together, they can form the starting point for a new type of national and transnational political action.

Some say that these plans are too general or too abstract, whereas what is needed is something more concrete, more current that can be achieved immediately. Given the circumstances, that general abstract quality doesn't seem like a bad thing. We need to throw open our windows, turn our gazes upward and look at the sky. We can't be narrow-minded; we need to be ambitious.

We can move from the general to the particular. But it is a mistake to think that one can do the reverse, to think that the particular can exist without the general, or that we can change things at the lower levels, but leave everything as it is at the upper levels. To do that would be to change nothing and lose everything. And if we do that, ultimately, we will lose our freedom.

If you wish to contribute, add to the list of potential plans or react to this book, please visit www.giuliotremonti.it.

Appendices

Appendix 1

A Few Papers from My Files

Letter from Minister Giulio Tremonti to Minister Christine Lagarde[23] *(September 29, 2008)*

Dear Christine,

After the American Congress vote . . . I would like to let you have my initial reactions given the urgency of the situation.

Above all, we cannot react to extraordinary circumstances with ordinary tools; it is not possible to face a new and truly uncertain reality with old tools, and we cannot think in local terms about these matters, which really have profoundly global origins and development. This is the reason I wish to put forward a few thoughts (from 1 to 4) so that we can confront the current crisis immediately together on a political level: This means *primum vivere* (survival first).

[23] French minister for the Economy, Industry and Work, from 2007 to 2011. (France held the presidency of the European Union in September 2008.)

Our market is a complex collection of elements in which transparency and confidence—which are tightly connected to one another—play a truly crucial role in terms of the strength of our economies. Unfortunately, at the moment, the only element which can truly be said to be growing is speculation; and that is the profound and dramatic antithesis of transparency as well as confidence. Therefore, we must act in haste to avoid further negative effects.

Only later will we truly be able to think about ways to avoid future crises and to work together to create a new situation that we want to (that we all must . . .) build. And we are definitely in agreement on the fact . . . that a new order certainly requires a wide consensus.

My proposals, in the meantime:

1) Accounting regulations are strategic. The rules that we have now are suicidal. It is therefore essential that we swiftly define a new system of accounting standards and rules.

2) In meeting this objective, a political agreement may be necessary in order to carry out a temporary delisting of the assets of banks, financial institutions and administrations involved in the crisis. I know that such a measure is very delicate for the markets. Therefore it should be decided upon and if necessary implemented in the most coordinated and efficient way possible.

3) We can agree on the new proposal . . . to create a pool of funds to avoid large liquidity crises. In so doing, we touch upon a point that should be in the forefront

of our minds at this time. We cannot give our publics the misleading impression that our actions are aimed principally at helping bankers and managers of financial institutions. In other words, we must clarify that our political wish, in implementing this specific measure, is not to make our citizens pay for the mistakes of others. What we wish to do and what we will do is to safeguard people's savings, and certainly not the interests of banks and institutions that have nearly obliterated these savings. It is with this same strong political desire that we must work to make concrete the idea, agreed upon at Nice after the Italian proposal, of a European Fund (through the EIB) that could help reinforce the European economy in strategic sectors. This is of increasing strategic importance politically speaking.

4) Speculation is one of the causes of the current situation. We must urgently announce on a political level that a set of simple measures—including through international institutions, such as the European Union—will be put in place to combat and contain it. Yet containment will certainly not be enough to satisfy the public. Again, on a political level, we must make clear that we are warning of the strong necessity of an enforcement system, and we must therefore imagine how we could begin to attack all the past, present, extraordinary and unjustified gains of speculators. We must urgently implement a simple and innovative system with this aim.

Once we have taken these important steps, we will certainly need to approve a catalogue of new general rules (financial transactions, commerce, transparency . . .). To this end, I am completely in agreement that it is important to begin to discuss this already in Washington, on the occasion of our G7 meeting, but I also propose that we meet—before work begins on the afternoon of Friday, the 10th—in a G4 plus Commission format, in order to better prepare for our discussions with our colleagues.

It really is a testing time. If we succeed, we will have the space and the desperate need to come up with a new political scenario.

Yours,

Giulio Tremonti

G7/G8 2009—Finance Ministers Draft Italian Program, a Few Proposals (Autumn 2008)

1) From the United States to Latin America, from Europe to Asia, the origin, the scale and the intensity of the crisis are global. If the crisis is global, then the solution cannot be local. The solution must be global, or it will not be a solution.

2) The current crisis is quite different from past ones. In a globalized world, it has an immediate impact on all countries, all markets and all societies. Even if the catalyst of the crisis was instability in the financial markets, the crisis is having an effect on the real economy, on people's well-being and on social, political and geopolitical stability.

3) New problems cannot be tackled with old solutions. It is inefficient and indeed dangerous to use conventional tools in exceptional situations.

4) Given the scale and the nature of the crisis, as just indicated, the solution cannot be technical: It must be institutional.

5) The current status quo of the G8 process is increasingly unsustainable. If the economy is global, an efficient structure of governance must also be global. The current G8 represents less than half of the world economy.

6) The "new G" must set the agenda for a new Bretton Woods to tackle fundamental issues, such as:

a) Exchange rates: The old Bretton Woods agreement for the balance of payments is showing its age, and the current crisis could offer an opportunity to create a new order.

b) Commercial flows: The Doha Round negotiations have reached a stalemate, but the crisis could provide an opportunity to establish clear commercial criteria.

c) Financial regulation: What we have is a flawed set of rules. They are rules typical of a financial capitalism with short-term orientation. They put everything at risk. It is absolutely essential to draw up as soon as possible a new set of regulations and accounting standards that would prohibit some contracts and instruments, hitting some specific countries if necessary.

d) Energy and climate change: This is an urgent and global problem. It therefore requires global action. Developed, emerging and developing economies should all be involved. In tackling climate change, we must bear in mind efficiency, efficacy and equity.

e) Development: We need new mechanisms in order to act more quickly and with more efficacy to help those who are most vulnerable. In doing so, we must widen our approach, listening to the growing number of people who are calling out for opportunity and who won't accept dependence any longer. We will continue, beyond specific projects and programs, to look for new ways to pursue development, also using innovative tools.

7) As the "new G" system will be complex, it will require a more permanent organization to sustain and

support its initiatives. The old Bretton Woods system, and in particular the International Monetary Fund and the World Bank, must be given a new mandate to offer a platform and to contribute to the implementation of such a process. The International Monetary Fund is in an ideal position to work on the coordination of new regulations and associated supervision. The Monetary Fund and the World Bank can also contribute to mobilize additional resources in order to tackle every possible evolution of the crisis. Both agencies enjoy a unique expertise in crucial sectors of the world economy. Moreover, their universal representation guarantees the Monetary Fund and the World Bank full legitimacy to speak on behalf of the international community.

Our political commitment consists of acting in the most multilateral way to transform the problems of our time, if possible, into opportunities.

A new European Fund to Promote Growth and Finance European Projects in the Energy and Infrastructure Sectors (September 2008)

A new plan of action is necessary to encourage growth in the European economy. A plan that must also represent a strong political message on the part of the European Union.

New instruments to finance investments in energy and infrastructure programs in Europe could contribute in part to overcoming the current economic and financial crisis.

To reach these objectives, Europe needs a new long-term vision. The paradigm of the political economy is changing. The short-term nature of financial capitalism is in part responsible for the current situation. We must return to a long-term continental European capitalism. In this way, the European Union can return to center stage with a strong political message, sustaining investments with broad horizons.

The economic and financial crisis and the risks of ungoverned globalization are putting the European community under a lot of pressure. There are widespread fears of a breach of social peace and a loss of economic well-being, jobs and access to housing in the present, but also for future generations. Political Europe must give new hope to its citizens. A political message, a great initiative for growth, a "sovereign" European response to a fear of a world order that is changing, is the principle necessity.

But how? Introducing new financial instruments that will not be a burden on national public finances and on future generations. Reuniting institutional European investors with a long-term horizon to sustain broad public-private initiatives . . . .

It is time to make better use of long-term institutional investors and their expertise in order to sustain public authorities.

Global institutional investors, such as pension funds and insurance companies, are in search of long-term, low-risk investments. Large European infrastructural projects with a stable cash flow and substantial institutional commitments have these characteristics. A European Fund for energy and infrastructure financed by European institutions such as the EIB, the CDC, the CDP, the KFW and other such bodies, would be able to attract other funds in the global financial arena. Size matters, and a large size necessitates a very abundant flow of investments.

The Proposal of a European Fund

The proposal:

1) open up the proprietary base of the European Investment Fund (EIF) to long-term institutional investors such as the Caisse des Dépots, the Cassa Depositi e Prestiti, KFW and other analogous European institutions;

2) extend the mission of the EIF to other sectors such as energy and infrastructure;

3) authorize a strong increase of capital to sustain these activities.

The EIF is a profit-oriented institution. In this it differs from the EIB, which is a policy-driven institution. The idea could be to make the CDC, CDP, KFW and other similar institutions acquire the amounts owned by private financial institutions (at a value of about 300 million euros) and give the Fund a new prudence-driven focus.

Perhaps this won't be enough. The size of the Fund should be increased substantially, on the strength of its new mission—to give greater support to the SMEs and enter into new sectors, such as energy and infrastructure. This could happen via a large increase in capital partially financed by national institutions with long-term goals.

This broadening of sectors of intervention could encompass, among others, the eco-energy industry, as defined by the Competitiveness and Innovation Framework Program (CIP) that is already part of the EIF's mission, along with nuclear energy (EURATOM).

A working committee could be created this week in Nice on the occasion of the informal Ecofin meeting, with the task of producing a report to discuss at the Ecofin of Finance Ministers in Brussels in November. Any proposals could then be put to European leaders at the European Council in December.

Appendix 2

Preface to the Japanese Edition of The Fear and the Hope *by Former Governor of the Bank of Japan Toshihiko Fukui*

In the past, when I was the governor of the Bank of Japan, I had the opportunity to work alongside Minister Giulio Tremonti at G7 meetings, and I still have today a vivid recollection of the seriousness with which he participated in discussions.

The common denominator in all of Minister Tremonti's proposals is the notion that in order to move toward a method of economic management that is adequate given the exigencies we face, one must not only muster the strength of the market, but also that of the political world.

Minister Tremonti, the author of this book, is extremely appreciated the world over for his profound erudition and skill in the tasks he carries out. *The Fear and the Hope* is full of ideas for the future that we truly hope will be realized one day. He is a key figure not only in Italian finance but also more widely in European financial affairs.

As his other works, written during the time of his

political activity (*Fatal Risks,* 2005; *The Ghost of Poverty*, 1995) demonstrate, Minister Tremonti is a person who believes strongly in a new order on a global scale.

Appendix 3

From the First Few Pages of The Fear and the Hope

What happened?[24] What happened is that in a very short amount of time, little more than ten years, the structure and the speed of the world have changed. Processes that would normally have taken up a longer chunk of history, spread over decades and decades, have been squashed into a small period and then have suddenly exploded. As we have already seen in so many other revolutions, globalization was prepared by intellectuals, put into place by fanatics, by crazy preachers with theological faith, searching for an earthly paradise.

The course of this particular history could certainly not have been stopped, but someone and something—and we shall see who and what—wished, insanely, for it to happen and caused an acceleration, opening up, like in the myth of Pandora's box, liberating and scattering forces which are now difficult to control. . . . Proceeding along an inevitable course of rupture, globalization is presenting us . . . with its bill, consisting of financial

[24] What follows, published in 2008, was written in 2007.

crisis and geopolitical tensions that, ready to erupt, are accumulating across the world. . . . When history comes to the end of one of its great cycles, we almost always find ourselves faced with the unexpected, the irrational, the obscure, the violent, and not always with good. The world has already been governed by demons on several occasions.

In Europe, for the majority of the population—not for the few at the top, but for the many who are at the bottom of the pyramid—earthly paradise, the increased well-being brought about by globalization only lasted for a short time, a couple of years. What should have been a social and environmental high-salaried paradise in fact turned into its opposite. It will get worse for those who have suffered the most and better for those already in a good situation. . . . It's not just a question of money. Because the guaranteed security of well-being that globalization was supposed to bring has been transformed into personal, social, general and environmental insecurity. . . . The second bill that globalization is currently handing us, after the shock effect on prices and a higher cost of living, is the "financial crisis" itself. A bill that, to tell the truth, globalization handed first to itself.

Under the pressure of the approaching crisis, the very alchemists who just yesterday (only at the end of the 20th century), invented "marketism," the mother-utopia of globalization, its excessively powerful ideological engine, are the first to be declaring themselves bankrupt. The shocks that have already been noted are enough to sink the fairy tale that economic progress would continue, for free, and they signal our sudden return from financial futurism to the difficulties of material reality; they impose the movement from irresponsibility to responsibility; they bring with them the end of the illusion that thanks to the new capitalism, profit can be extracted instantaneously from debt bonds whose origins and bases are unknown, or from ownership bonds that don't exist concretely, like in the virtual reality of a video game; finally, in a time of crisis, they put an end to globalization's development mechanism. Globalization and finance are in fact two sides of the same coin. Globalization and finance have been partners since the beginning, and suddenly began to live in symbiosis. . . . Globalization, with the opening of vast spaces of the market and the collapse of old boundaries and old controls, forged the new finance. The new finance, permitting a division of the world into an Asia that produces low cost goods and a debt-ridden America that consumes, has in turn pushed and "doped" globalization, far outstripping, with its huge fantastical numbers, the smaller, more concrete numbers of the real economy. Over the last ten years, with a market acceleration in the last five in particular, within the banking industry and therefore at the heart of the new marketist capitalism, there has been a super-strong double mutation, large in terms of its size and the role that it plays. A sizeable mutation: The large international banks, going through a process of global concentration, have at last taken the dominant form of "megabanks." A functional mutation, because the megabanks have applied a new form of techno-finance, the Originate-to-Distribute (OTD) model in a radical way and on a global scale. The OTD is not only a new operating technique that permits the "distribution" of credit risk, with the transferal of the risk itself from the original creditor bank to a third one. It is something more than that, something that has the capacity to create a new type of bank: a bank that is at once universal and irresponsible. In this way, universality and irresponsibility have become the ultimate characteristics of the megabank, a completely new type of industry. For centuries, the banks have in fact taken money on trust and lent it at their own risk, the art of the banker lying essentially in the ability to value the merit of "own risk," which is adopted and then managed. In a crescendo beginning more or less at the beginning of the century, the century of globalization, the open structure of the financial markets, the collapse of control and new financial techniques have instead all permitted a way out from this fixed scheme: the rupture of the old balance between risk and responsibility; the opening of a stark asymmetry between the origin of the risk and the responsibility for the risk. And so new global megabanks have freed themselves from the original risk of their loans, transferring the risk to a third party. They did this by packaging their credits in financial products, sometimes called bonds, which were in turn given another name. All were destined to be linked on the market through buyers attracted by high revenues, confused by the complexity of the instruments and almost always unaware of the risk of these "junk securities" that they were thereby taking on.

Everything developed under a perverse fewer-risks-more-gains mechanism, because, with new financial technologies, the more operators transferred their risk to third parties, the more profits they made. The so-called subprimes, risky loans permitted in the SA and then packaged up and circulated, along with associated risks, around the world, were in reality the first link in a very long chain of escaping risk and seeking profit. An escape and a search undertaken with many other instruments: credit default swaps, vehicles, conduits, asset-backed commercial papers, collateralized debt obligations, derivatives, monolines, hedge funds, etc. Instruments that differed from one another but always had a common denominator: They were operated and operable beyond any kind of control. The hedge funds—for example—are nothing but irregular banks. The opposite of the old banks. The banks are in fact subject to state jurisdiction, to prudential regulations, standards, limits and criteria governing their actions. This is not the case when it comes to hedge funds. Their regulation consists of one single rule: that there are no rules. It is precisely in this way that hedge funds became the opposite of what their own name suggests (hedge = anti-risk coverage). The combination of these new forms of techno-finance has injected huge quantities of liquidity into the market, and this in turn was multiplied with debt leverage. This is how the values of operations rose artificially. Values that were mostly invented, financed by debt, with no risk to the individual but to a third party instead. With one particularity. In Asia, the instrument of debt is used in a traditional way, to finance the construction of new industries, while in the West, in the spectacular crescendo of the last few years, the same instrument has instead been used to finance consumption and to speculate on the value of already existing industries, not to create new ones.

This is how the megabanks, which have become both universal and irresponsible, artificially replicating and multiplying values, potentially to the nth degree, benefiting from more or less solid insurance coverage and auditing certification, benefiting from the positive grading awarded them by the ratings agencies, ended up with hundreds of billions of dollars and euros of their own assets, upon which they issued derivatives mounting to thousands of billions of dollars and euros, on their books. This was something totally new and yet frighteningly similar to the old bad checks. Something that affects and distorts not only the profit and loss sheets, but also and above all the balance sheets, which came to reflect not only what a megabank earned in a year, but also the total assets of the same megabank. Something potentially resembling a global Parmalat.

This is how the countermodel became the model, the exception became the rule, negativity the standard.

Only now are governments denouncing, in the most authoritative of terms, the high level of complexity of these new instruments. But this very complexity should have and could have been the first and clearest proof of the substantial uselessness and danger of instruments configured into something resembling indecipherable financial hieroglyphics!

All of this means that in the end, the bad practices of some have become everyone's fear. And so, under the mechanism of the crisis taking place, the bankers no longer trust the bankers (G. Tremonti, *I banchieri non si fidano piu dei banchieri*, ["The bankers no longer trust the bankers"], *Corriere della Sera*, September 21, 2007). In this way the vital inter-bank circuit has been reduced to the point of disappearing. This circuit works within capitalism as the circulation system works within the body. The authorities and the central banks ought now to replace it with an impressive series of public interventions, never before so extensive in size and duration, so as to publicly announce the intention of working in this way until there have been enough replacement interventions. Until when, then? It has been written, hastily and reductively, that what is happening at the moment is not a crisis of liquidity but *only* a crisis of confidence. In reality, saying that there is liquidity in the financial market but no confidence is like saying that there is a Church temporarily without any faith! The idea of beating the crisis with a new Operation Truth, based on the writing of new and clearer accounting regulations

(G. Tremonti, "The bankers no longer trust the bankers") was naturally not even taken into consideration. History does, after all, repeat itself. Following the crisis of 1929, in respect of the idea to introduce "institutions, and norms of behavior whose functional and temporal horizon goes beyond single interest of individuals" into the system, the preferred idea was to place more confidence "in those who fabricated and sold paper across half the world . . . using a paper switch similar to those that caused the crisis in the first place." (Luigi Einaudi, writing about the 1929 crisis in *Il Mio piano non è quello di Keynes* ["My plan isn't the Keynes plan,"] 1933). Thus the continuing opacity inherent in the financial market generated a lack of confidence and it is now this lack of confidence that is fuelling the crisis, which appears to us to be a crisis of globalization. As discussed, the new techno-finance was not merely an updated means to carry out the classic financial speculations of the past. It was something absolutely new. Something never seen before on this scale. Creating the effects of wealth and artificial demand, the new techno-finance has in fact been fundamental in financing the almost instantaneous "miracle" of globalization. What we cannot say is that after August 2007, the worst is over, and nothing so bad can or could happen again. It is not imprudent to expect more extreme happenings. Other shocks. Because, as in a cascade of phenomena, a chain that links causes and effects, which in turn become the causes of other effects, the financial crisis can intersect with other forces and powers. It can intersect with political imbalances caused by the new imperialism or by political chaos, typical in countries that export energy and are areas of mineral cultivation. But in any case, what has already happened is enough in itself and advances by pushing us towards different mental horizons than the ones that have until now been dominant, towards a different vision of life, less material and more spiritual, less enclosed within the private sphere and laissez-faire principles, more community minded, more responsible, that is to say, more political. This is the heralded "return of the public." The economy is important, but reality in its fullness and life in its complexity are another matter altogether.

Appendix 4

The Twenty Years That Changed the Structure and Speed of the World

What happened?

Flash back. Everything started in Europe, with the fall of the Berlin Wall. And it only took twenty years, from 1989 to 2009. Those twenty years saw a change in the structure and the speed of the world.

Of course, what we're experiencing was long ago bound to happen, a development that has its roots in the beginning of the 20th century, in America, in Africa and in Asia.

But it was only in 1989 that time really began to compress until suddenly, it exploded. Never in the history of humanity has such a change taken place in so short a time.

Certainly the geographical discovery of America in the middle of the previous millennium perturbed Europe's closed isolation, destroyed the basis of the feudal system and brought new religions and techniques into play. However, it took at least two centuries for the full effects of this phenomenon to be revealed.

By contrast, the economic discovery of Asia did not

take such a typically lengthy period of time, did not adopt the slow rhythm of transition from one generation to the next. On the contrary, it took a very short amount of time, shorter than the average person's lifetime—it took twenty years. What happened in those years?

November 9, 1989: the fall of the Berlin Wall, the end of communism in an area artificially divided from the world for almost half a century. *April 15, 1994*: the World Trade Organization (WTO) treaty is signed in Marrakech, Morocco. The creation of a new, balanced, mercantile agreement, going beyond geopolitical boundaries. *December 11, 2001*: China becomes a member of the WTO. *Summer 2007*: the first global financial crisis begins. At the time of this writing it is the end of 2011.

The process that developed over these years is for the most part based on a mix of these five fundamental factors:

a) A geopolitical factor: with the fall of the Berlin Wall, the axis of American political power shifted from the Atlantic to the Pacific.

b) A technical factor: the diffusion and application of information technology.

c) An economic factor: the foremost division of the world—Asia, producer of low-cost goods, America, buyer of debt.

d) A financial factor: the new techno-finance, which, using the fluid magic of new money, banking and virtual money, facilitated the instantaneous miracle of globalization.

e) An ideological factor: a synthesis of all of the above: marketism. The ultimate totalitarian ideology of the 1900s. The political divination of the market. For centuries in Europe, politics was nationally dominated by the triad of "Liberté, Égalité, Fraternité." Globalization deluded us, however, that this old triad could be replaced by a new one: "Globalité, Marché, Monnaie," inscribed on the imposing frontispiece of the new temple to the market god.

It is precisely in these terms that we can see the cause and effect relationship that has developed between globalization (the cause) and the crisis (the effect). Globalization could certainly not be stopped, and it was—it is—fundamentally a positive thing. Yet from a historical perspective, the timing of globalization and the methods by which it came into being could have been more carefully considered and drawn out. Perhaps then we could have avoided the crisis. Perhaps. But what we now have in front of us is the reality. This is the material structure of our existence.

We can only take note, philosophically observing that it is globalization that has made Marx's prophecy come true: "The old national independence will be superseded by a global interdependence."

Just a few years, not even a century ago, the common trend was very very different. It was a trend not to see crises as crises, but instead to treat them as cycles; to downplay them, considering them only "turbulence in the financial markets"; to exorcise them, to see so-called decoupling on the horizon (whereby the old economies are stalling, but the new ones are making up for it by accelerating).

The crisis is, however, general and global. General in its impact, because it is not limited to finance (the first stage), but extends to the real economy (the second stage) and from there ultimately extends, or could extend to social and political structures, changing lifestyles, but not for the better, and it could begin to have an influence on elections and to cause violent, new social disorder (the third stage).

It is global, by extension, because it could spread from the United States to Asia, from Europe to Russia and to Latin America.

This isn't a sufficiently complete analysis. The relationship between crisis and globalization is in fact a double relationship: not only is the crisis global, but, as we've seen, it originates from globalization. The relationship between crisis and globalization cannot be reduced into a simple juxtaposition based on the classic logical fallacy of *post hoc, ergo propter hoc* (after this, therefore because of this).

The relationship between these two, crisis and globalization, is causal rather than casual. A rationally mechanical relationship, a cause-and-effect relationship. Globalization was not and is not an entirely natural phenomenon, but rather a phenomenon with a political cause. A phenomenon of high political intensity.

This is why, because of its design and its political

dynamic, we must look to globalization to find the cause of the crisis: the crisis is global because it has causes that are themselves global.

Globalization has been, is and certainly will be a great, positive opportunity for humanity. Yet it has been and—I repeat—still is the origin of huge imbalances and gravely critical situations. Not, perhaps, globalization in itself, but the way it has been directed politically: too hurriedly, I say, and with too much debt.

Too much of a hurry. Throughout history, the opening up of large spaces, the elimination of physical distances has repeatedly caused ruptures in systems.

This was true of the geographical discovery of America, centuries ago. It was true a few years ago, with the economic discovery of Asia.

With one difference: the first was a natural fact, a geographical discovery. The second was instead political. The first was a process that took a least a few centuries to reach its historical fulfillment. The second was instead an instantaneous phenomenon.

Hugely important processes normally take place within long-lasting cycles, the cycle characteristic of Tacitus' *Annals*. The time that it takes to pass from one generation to another. Not a tiny moment in time, concentrated within the average span of a human life.

Twenty years separate 1989 from today, or rather, from 2009: first ten years of preparation, then ten years of explosion. In a historical sense, it really is hardly any time at all.

It's not just that. Not only was globalization carried

out too hastily, but more long-term and balanced political methods should have been applied. Methods that could have reduced the impact of enormous economic, social, cultural and political discrepancies that are typical of such an intense phenomenon as globalization. Pandora's box could be and needed to be opened, but much more carefully.

What's more, globalization was also brought about with too much debt, because it was based upon a primary division of the world, with Asia as the producer of low-cost goods and America as the buyer of debt. A double debt. An internal debt because it is created in America under a special monetary policy that creates artificial values based on real estate values. A policy based on what were called subprime mortgages. In addition, there is also external debt, contracted with Asia by America itself. Asia participates first as the seller of its goods and then, symmetrically, as the buyer of American public bonds.

This explains why the heart of the crisis lies in the financial sector and, specifically, in the logic of debt.

In earlier decades, this was the way the degeneration of capitalism began, and as a result began to configure our society into a new sort of society: a debt society, of a leveraged society.

The simultaneously euphoric and paroxysmal function of debt encouraged the use of debt instruments to do more than acquire growing quantities and surpluses of private consumer goods. Debt was used not only to construct new industrial goods but also to acquire ownership of industrial goods that were already in existence (new debt for old structures), creating, in the end, paper wealth.

The degeneration of capitalism then consequently manifested itself in four main malfunctions:

First malfunction. For centuries, bankers have gathered money on trust and lent money at their own risk, evaluating the risk and then assuming the responsibility for it. The new financial method has in fact permitted those who gather the money to free themselves of risk and to do so by selling the risk to a third party incorporating it into new financial products. Fewer risks and more gains. And so the risk began to circulate. There was a lot of literature predicting that these derivatives would have a positive function, of progressive reduction, amortization, a cancellation of the risk. Almost everybody would benefit, even the citizens of India. In short, according to this literature, derivatives would constitute a new and positive social discovery. As if the great social discovery of the 1800s, the progressive tax, would be followed by a new discovery, exactly equivalent in terms of having a purely socially positive function: derivative finance.

This led to a breakdown in models of behavior. There's an old saying: Banks will lend you money like they'd lend you an umbrella. Except they only lend it to you when there's good weather and they take it away again when the rain comes. Here the opposite happened:

debt followed by more debt. This is how it became quite normal to live in debt, thanks to the kind hearts of the banks, during the progression of a paradigm that, based on the mathematized gambling of derivatives, created and is creating a crisis.

Second malfunction. The opportunity to develop economic and financial activities (the new emerging and high-performance capitalism) outside of ordinary jurisdiction. It has been said that this type of degenerative evolution of capitalism is due to so-called deregulation. As we'll see later, that's not the only thing behind it.

The essence of the problem lies not only in deregulation, which, I repeat, does play a fundamental role, but also in the opportunity to develop activity outside of all types of jurisdiction. The world's new geopolitical structure has permitted a sort of shopping for legislation, allowing the development of activities not only in areas characterized by a real, ordinary jurisdiction—real in the sense of being both formal and substantial—but also in areas formally organized into jurisdictions, but where in substance, the only rule was (is) that there aren't any rules. In this way, a huge proportion of capitalism, a greater proportion than that permitted free reign by deregulation, entered the realm of anomy, the chosen habitat of so-called shadow finance.

Third malfunction. Capitalism is essentially based on the typical scheme, the ideal type, of the corporation. Capitalism generated the joint-stock corporation through its actions and vice versa, just as in the example of the chicken and the egg. It was on the back of the corporation that capitalism developed the system of stability it greatly needs. The system of jurisdictional, administrative, media and judicial controls was in turn based on the workings of the joint-stock corporation—up until a few years ago, when the most affluent, dynamic and high-performance part of capitalism moved away from the corporate model and began to use other instruments: hedge funds, equity funds. These instruments represent an absolutely foreign and alternative evolution with respect to the basic legal model of capitalism, which is that of the joint-stock corporation.

Fourth malfunction. Capitalism and, within capitalism, the joint-stock corporation, are based (among other things) on the fundamental technical criterion of double-entry. The double-entry criterion is organized basically and fundamentally on the distinction between a balance sheet and a profit and loss account. One does not exist without the other. However, recent capitalism has freed itself from the restraints of double-entry. It has shifted to the profit and loss account only, abandoning the balance sheet. This was in some ways an accounting decision, but above all a political and moral one. The balance sheet represents in fact the world of values. The profit and loss account instead represents the world of prices. The balance sheet is a world in which the structure, history, origins, present and future of a corporation can be seen, along with its moral and industrial mission. The profit and loss account is another thing altogether. If all of capitalism turns towards profit and loss accounts and ceases to be guided by long-term logic, as is typical and characteristic of the balance sheet, if it becomes short-sighted, brief, as is the logic of the profit and loss account, if it no longer considers the duration of a corporation, but only the business year, which in turn is divided into six-month periods, quarters, daily fixing, then it is clear that everything has changed. So capitalism has taken on the form of the profit and loss account and is beginning gradually to configure a new type of capitalism, a sort of "take-away" capitalism. You take wealth from the balance sheet, you strip it of its value, and then you carry it off.

It is through each of these four malfunctions that financial mutation of capitalism has come about in such a revolutionary way.

Appendix 5

The Financial Stability Board

The Financial Stability Forum (FSF) was established in 1999 at the behest of the G7.

The FSF brought together all the national authorities of the great financial centers and international bodies responsible for setting standards, such as the International Organisation of Securities Commissions (IOSCO), the Basel Committee on Banking Supervision (BCBS), the International Association of Insurance Supervisors (IAIS) and the International Accounting Standards Board (IASB).

Initially, the FSF functioned as a forum for the coordination and exchange of information, a sort of debate club discussing the ideal ways to organize finance. A forum that prided itself on the financial world, adding to the Compendium of Standards a collection of abstract principles to make markets function well.

However, the explosion of the crisis brutally demonstrated that *that* finance was not the best finance possible, above all because of the absence of rules.

It was in that context that an attempt was made to

improve quality, to introduce dozens of organizational and institutional changes and revisions. Thus the G20, at its first summit in 2008 and then in April 2009, decided to modify the FSF according to geographical representation and areas of interest and rechristened it the Financial Stability Board (FSB) in order to indicate its strategic novelty.

Membership on the rechristened Financial Stability Board was extended to all the G20 countries, Spain and the European Commission. Its mandate was reinforced by the explicit allocation of responsibilities for various financial topics, including the following areas: regulation and control of all financial institutions deemed important from a systemic point of view; the revision of regulatory systems, including the consideration of macro-prudential risks; fighting jurisdictions that do not cooperate in exchanging information; development of capital adequacy of the international banking system; subjecting the ratings agencies to regulation; and the working out of guidelines for remuneration of the managers of financial institutions.

This strategy is plain to see in the decision of the first G20 summit, held in Washington in November 2008. The FSB was promoted, effective immediately, from being an amusing conversation circle to being the savior of newly created finance. In the attachment to the memo, this cathartic mission was meticulously broken down into 38 specific tasks (out of 42 indicated on the original document), then elaborated on further, as

I noted earlier, for a total of 16,000 pages, in a text 80 kilometers long.

Instead of acting decisively on the excessive assumption of risk and on all the other instances of negligence and abuse in the financial world, the FSB and the Basel Committee turned their attention to the capital adequacy of the main financial institutions, the so-called SIFIs (Systemically Important Financial Institutions).

Under normal circumstances, it is true as well as banal to say that an adequate amount of capital used to counteract physiological losses is necessary in order for a bank to have solidity.

The crisis, however, is not a physiological one. It is a serious symptom of the system. Too much risk, too much liquidity, too much financial leverage with increasingly complex and dangerous instruments. Instead of considering and confronting the causes, they turned to capital requirements, working on the assumption that with more capital, the financial sector would, independently of its own behavior, become more solid, with fewer losses and fewer costs to the taxpayer.

This is not the case. It's all in the facts. So far, greater capital has translated into greater losses, not smaller ones.

Risk capital is actually a notional category. What matters is how, and how productively, available finances are committed, meaning the quality of the assets and the assumption of risks within the limits of what is reasonable. To be sure that what happens demonstrates above all that activities comply with monitoring and regulation.

Excessively aggravating the restrictions of capital can not only be *useless*, but also *damaging*, in a time of crisis, because it pushes the banks not so much to raise their own funds but more to reduce credit, the credit offered to small- and medium-sized businesses in particular, and to mobilize the government bonds with the most volatile prices, independently of the causes of variability. And so the vicious circle continues. A circle that does not manage even to avoid the long transitory period foreseen for the implementation of Basel III. The operators anticipate the new restrictions and from then on aim to contract a credit portfolio that bad trends will make more risky. Few or none of those hit are the actual operators, who consider finance to work like a casino (a casino they own—they're not gambling with their own money certainly) either because they are not regulated, or because the capital and liquidity requirements of Basel III and the FSB govern neither hedge funds nor merchant banks. Indeed, precisely because of the delimitations of their field of jurisdiction, the new rules push activity toward these unmonitored areas.

A false logic also underpins the imposition of greater capital requirements for systemic institutions (SIFIs) that are very large and structured so as to render the thought of failure impossible: too big to fail. More stringent restrictions on capital—this is the idea—make the large institutions more solid, and therefore allow taxpayers to sleep peacefully.

This, in reality, is how new perverse incentives are created. Once the token clamor over unjust discrimination is finished, the SIFIs in fact adhere to the norms and find full justification for continuing legitimately in the unregulated assumption of risks. Having paid for a "license to kill," they have still fewer scruples about their behavior and as systemic institutions they continue to have their backs covered by the taxpayer as shareholders of last resort. If Basel III is a capital sin, the others cannot be pardoned. Meanwhile the FSB continues with its other tasks, which are varied and innumerable but have one thing in common: irrelevance and inconclusiveness.

No concrete reform has been outlined in terms of the regulation and monitoring of shadow banking. Yet this is a fundamental question. One of the most major causes of the crisis is in fact this long undisturbed operation, which takes place in an obscure galaxy of atypical brokers, and is about *double* the size of the banking sector in the United States and equal to about half the world's banking activity. Disintermediation and regulatory arbitrage serve to make the assumption of risk even more explosive.

Progress on derivatives reform has also been scarce, more or less limited to the standardization of over-the-counter (OTC) derivatives; the fight against noncooperative jurisdictions, the definition of guidelines for the commodities derivatives market and the regulation of shadow banking have still not produced concrete results.

Another technique to reduce the capacity to influence

the behavior of markets and financial operators is the great freedom with which the necessary transposition of agreements of domestic regulations can take place. The huge flexibility with which standards and principles are accepted (for example, regulations on the remuneration of financial managers) compromises the effectiveness of the reforms and poses serious problems for regulatory arbitrage.

These delays reveal the persistence of the causes at the heart of the crisis. The financial industry's ability to exert pressure remains unchanged in the Anglo-Saxon area as well as in the bodies responsible for defining standards (the standard setting bodies). These bodies have been taken over by the financial industry and they dominate the governance of the FSB. Many of the negotiations, beginning with those over Basel III, revolve around these bodies. Deep within the FSB, the political authorities (finance ministers) are in a clear minority compared to the technical authorities, and they are wholly absent from the Directive Committee, the subgroup that effectively makes all the important decisions. Just like its predecessor, the FSB has continued to operate as a bankers' club.

This is not altered by the fact that membership of the FSB has been extended, more in form than in substance, to emerging countries. The FSB considers matters that are typical of advanced countries. In this sense, emerging countries only have the chance to prevent decisions from being made that could be potentially damaging for them.

The FSB wants to consolidate and strengthen itself further, giving as justification the considerable burden of work it has been assigned. According to plans, this would impose a review of its internal workings and its organizational structure, only two years after it rose from the ashes of the FSF.

At the behest of the G20, several proposals have been put forward for strengthening the FSB, focusing on governance, internal processes and the need for resources.

The most relevant of these proposals concern: the review of the composition of the FSB Steering Committee, which currently does not include representatives from finance ministries; the reinforcement of working methods to secure a more transparent circulation of information between the members and more efficient work from the FSB Plenary; and, above all, the recognition of FSB budget autonomy currently financed by the EIB budget, which would represent a likely irreversible step toward formally making the FSB a new international financial institution. With this aim, a Budget and Resource Committee has been created, to define its structure. Without limits, the force and strength of the FSB, a strength that derives from the binomial that defines it, manage to succeed in defending the interests of finance, and continue to fail to put an end to the crisis.

Appendix 6

Credit Default Swaps

From 2004 to 2010 the growth rate in the notional value of over-the-counter derivatives was 132%, while the expansion of CDS happened three times more quickly at 367%. Between 2004 and 2007 in particular, that is to say until the beginning of the subprime crisis, the CDS market grew to eight times its original size, confirming the highly speculative nature that this product had assumed.

While the underlying market has its own dimensions, and above it monetary authorities and large financial institutions act (or should act) in a regulatory context, the over-the-counter market is instead by definition opaque and without rules. With a reduced amount of resources, it is thus possible to agitate the volatility of the CDS spreads, provoking an imitative effect in the spreads of the underlying bonds. It's not just by chance that the spread of the former is always larger that that of the latter, which still tends to move in the same direction: The CDS function like a sort of bulldozer.

As stated earlier, in the past the CDS, in their original insurance function, had a positive role, because credit default swap quotes correctly signaled the growing risk in the market. Then everything changed. The choice of examples here is huge. For example, CDS played a key role in the collapse of Bear Stearns, one of the first American financial institutions to topple due to the effects of the crisis. Bear Stearns specialized in issuing asset back securities, that is, the bonds linked to subprime loans. When the real estate market begin to feel the effects, starting in 2006 and continuing through 2007, the spread on the Bear Stearns bonds rose progressively to 150 points, casting doubt on the real solidity of the company.

Up until then the CDS were just doing honest work. But they then became very damaging. The speculative attack on Bear Stearns came from them: Over the course of two months, between January and mid-March, the spread skyrocketed from 170 to 770 points, pushing the bank into a liquidity crisis that, due to the impossibility of sustaining itself on the capital market, quickly transformed into a solvency crisis. On March 14, 2008, the Federal Reserve of New York attempted a bailout, announcing a loan of 25 billion dollars to keep the bank running. But surrender was inevitable, and J.P. Morgan acquired Bear Stearns, paying just 2 dollars per share for shares that were valued at 133 dollars each before the crisis.

Given the huge profits that are made through CDS, no one seems able to, or has the political will to bring mutant CDS back under control, CDS which have played and still consequently play a central role in the growth of global systemic risk, which in turn led to the financial storm of 2008 and recently detonated the European sovereign debt crisis. The absence of regulation and transparency in negotiations has favored and continues to favor the use of CDS as an accelerator of financial instability.

The operating procedures peculiar to CDS must be added here. Through this instrument—as noted earlier—it is in fact possible to acquire a fire insurance policy relating to your neighbor's house, without indeed owning your neighbor's house. That is to say, it is possible to gamble on the creditworthiness of a company or a state without necessarily possessing the underlying fixed-rate security. This is what is know as a naked CDS: The only intention of the person who acquires one is in fact to gamble speculatively on the bankruptcy of the debtor—whether it be a company or sovereign state—in such a way as to maximize financial leverage and their own profit, too.

Of course, it does not have to get to the stage where the debtor defaults: To make money you just need to gamble on a deterioration in creditworthiness. Given that the spread applied to a CDS inversely correlates to the creditworthiness of the debtor, a contract acquired at a lower spread can subsequently be balanced against the sale of a similar contract at a higher spread. The speculator thus earns on the basis of the difference between the two payment flows, the smaller one, which pays out as the buyer of the protection, and the larger one, which collects as the provider of the protection.

Naked CDS represent a huge majority of the contracts now in circulation, which is in line with the clearly speculative nature of credit default swaps in general: The CDS investor has nothing to protect and every reason to play. If you add to this the fact that the contract dealers are not obliged to maintain special liquidity reserves or to respect the limits of capital requirements and if you observe that several contracts can be stipulated on the notional value of one bond, amplifying the risks that come from a possible default on the part of the debtor, you have a better idea of the financial danger of CDS. And the fact that the European Commission recently attempted to bring naked CDS under control, but only in Europe and not in the United States, speaks volumes not only about the resistance to that idea, but also about the slowness of the authorities.

This containment strategy applied to CDS, given the damage created by this type of derivative, is perhaps the first sign that the authorities are beginning to feel some regret. The alternate proposal, put forward by the FSB and aimed at standardizing CDS, creating one single global technological platform, where CDS would have to be placed, is a completely different matter, however. An innovation of this kind can be compared to the invention of the trench in World War I. Just as trenches did not prevent war, but instead prolonged it, so a new platform for CDS would not impede the crisis, but would expand it.

Appendix 7

Basel III

It is estimated that, during the transition to Basel III, the new rules will cost the banking system 30 to 50 billion euros in additional expenses in the eurozone, such as collecting money. Such charges will obviously be offloaded through the interest rates that the banks charge families and businesses, which results in an amount that is larger than the current cost of the money.

From a macroeconomic perspective, the direct consequences will be minimal, however GDP growth is expected to slow in the medium term from –0.05% to 0.15% a year. Forecasting a downturn of 0.05% in GDP is more complicated than trying to count a millipede's feet; aside from these econometric exercises, a banal truth remains: If the cost of money rises, then business investments will be affected, and the household consumption demand and eventually growth will be negatively affected at a time when there is very little growth as it is.

Stationing guards to monitor capital is not only costly but can sometimes be useless and thus dangerous. Let's take the case of Dexia, the great Franco-Belgian bank that collapsed in October 2011. Four months previously, this institution had not only received an excellent evaluation from the ratings agencies, but it had also been subjected to the stress tests carried out by the European Banking Authority and had acquitted itself admirably: Its base capital (Core Tier One) was close to 10.4%, almost double the amount demanded by the new and more stringent requirements of Basel III. The problem is that no financial institution can guard against a liquidity crisis and excessive recourse to leverage. The Dexia affair is therefore a window into the future of our banks: in the Basel era (of Basels III, IV, V, etc.) they will happily continue to collapse and according to the plans, to be bailed out with taxpayer cash.

But if Basel III does have a talent, it's for applying medicine to the wrong body part. This is where the final joke lies. The origin of the crisis was in America, in its banking system. But the American banks, which have already applied or not applied Basel II, are not very easy to subject to the regulations of Basel III. Naturally, there was an official statement pledging commitment to swiftly adopting the new agreement. But the rules governing banks are made by the banks. And the boss of a large bank has already declared that the new regulations are anti-American. As Samuel Johnson said, patriotism is the last refuge of a scoundrel. Recall that the FSB declared itself to be in total agreement with Basel III.

Appendix 8

The Ratings Agencies

It is probable that this very European offensive against the ratings agencies, which has, however, not gotten any further than mere resolutions, originated as a reaction to the particular severity with which the guardians of credit have been analyzing the debts of European sovereign states, despite the fact that many of the countries subjected to repeated downgrading have made great progress toward rebalancing their public finances.

This kind of severity certainly was not applied to Lehman Brothers in 2008, which suddenly went from triple A to default, precipitating the subprime crisis into a global economic crisis. Perhaps the changing judgment criteria are of a mercantile nature, given that Lehman, as a private entity, reimbursed the agency richly for its rating services, while the assassination of states is free of charge.

In the past, the ratings agencies did worse when interest rates were lower and so returns on high quality stocks were also low. In search of more attractive levels of performance, the creators of financial products began to construct complex, so-called structured stocks or securities, made up of *parts* of high-quality bonds and junk stocks, which were unreliable but provided large returns.

What was the aim of this? To combine high ratings with high returns. In tweaking these sausage stocks, as they've been termed, the issuers worked side by side with the rating agencies to calibrate the best possible dosages. We know how it ended. The crisis of confidence that assailed the financial markets transformed those sausage stocks into waste paper, because once the filling was ground up and stuffed into its casing, it was no longer possible to distinguish the good part from the bad part and so to assign it a market price.

The ratings agencies survived, therefore, and today they sit again in austere judgment over debt and no one—who knows why?—has yet thought to effectively regulate their activities. Regulations that should begin with a simple observation: In the real world, it isn't the person who's selling but the person who's acquiring who hires (and pays) a consultant, for the very good reason that the purchaser will be shelling out the cash. If I were going to buy a house, I'd have my own advisor decide the value, not the seller's advisor.

The conflict of interest between agencies and issuers is considerable, but it's not the only such conflict. The companies that ask for and finance the study that leads to a rating can in fact demand that it not be published. This leads to an informational imbalance, which can lead to phenomena such as insider trading and favor speculative behavior. To put it bluntly, delays in the provision of information can mean that bonds are bought and sold before their ratings are published and create a positive or negative effect.

Yet another source of danger lies in the strongly oligo-political structure of the ratings industry. You need only bear in mind that, according to recent estimates, the so-called Big Three control about 90% of the market and produce more than 2 billion dollars in profit each year. This situation favors nontransparent behavior, as can be noted in the fact that a downgrading (or indeed upgrading) announced on behalf of one of the three agencies is often followed by an adjustment in the same direction on the part of the other two.

Finally, it is worth asking what the ownership structures of these harsh judges are like. They are in some measure public companies, in the sense that no one individual shareholder can hold back the absolute majority of an agency. Yet it should be noted that, for some reason, the largest investment funds appear regularly on the lists of major shareholders of these agencies.

Appendix 9

The Statistics of the Common European Market

Normally it is said that emerging markets, with millions of potential consumers, are a veritable El Dorado for European businesses that can sell them their good and services.

Perhaps this will be the case in the future. It is not so at the moment and won't be in the near future either. The majority of European exports are in reality Europe to Europe, from one European country to another (or to the three traditional large wealthy non-European markets: the United States, Switzerland and the OPEC countries).

In 2010, the overall export of goods, Europe to Europe (plus those to the United States, Switzerland and the OPEC countries) represented the following proportion of total exports for the following countries: Germany 74.1%, France 75.6%, Italy 73.3% and the United Kingdom 73.3%.

Within these proportions about 60% is Europe to Europe. These percentages, which are extraordinarily close to each other, demonstrate especially that, as far as commercial trade concerned (and further on, we will see that this applies to financial transactions as well), the great European economies are predominantly and vitally connected to one another.

Meanwhile, the amount of exports to emerging markets, while increasing, is still secondary. It is therefore apparent that an aggravation of the crisis in Europe (and in the United States) would cause stark depressive relapse effects in the real economy.

More in-depth analysis can be read below:

Germany. In 2010, German exports stood at 957 billion euros, with a commercial surplus of 152.4 billion.

The idea that Germany has far outclassed all other advanced countries in penetrating emerging markets is very widespread. In reality, the European Union still represents 60.4% of Germany's exports, while the three most important traditional non-European nonemerging markets (again, the United States, Switzerland and the OPEC countries) constitute another 13.7%. In total, 74.1% of exports from Germany are concentrated within the European Union and in the three most important nonemerging and non-European markets. The most dynamic emerging market, China, absorbs only 5.6% of German exports (53.5 billion euros), which is less than exports to China from France (90.6 billion), the United Kingdom (59.3 billion), Italy (58.4 billion) and even Austria (53.7 billion).

The same four so-called peripheral countries (Portugal, Ireland, Greece and Spain), which German public opinion considers deadwood, a weight pulling down the economies of Germany and "virtuous" northern Europe, have export markets that are not unimportant to Germany: In 2010, Germany exported 50.1 billion euros in goods to these four countries, a little less than Germany exports to China!

It is particularly useful to analyze the composition of Germany's substantial commercial assets. The data shows that, even more than exports, the German trade surplus derives from exchanges with European countries and with rich countries, rather than with emerging countries. In 2010 in particular, out of 152.4 billion euros of foreign commercial assets, 65.9 were with the European Union and 58.9 were with the non-European, nonemerging markets (32.2 billion of which was with the United States). In total the European Union plus the three main nonemerging non-European markets represent about 82% (124.8 billion) of German commercial surplus.

With the four peripheral European countries, in 2010 Germany presented trade assets of 16.4 billion euros, while with China it showed a trade deficit of 9.9 billion dollars.

In 2010, Germany's four main export partners were, in order, France, the United States, the United Kingdom and Italy.

France. In 2010, France's exports totaled 393.3 billion euros, with a trade deficit of 64.7 billion.

The European Union represented 60.9% of the destinations of French exports, while the three most important non-European, nonemerging markets (United States, Switzerland and OPEC countries) made up another 14.1% of exports from Paris. In total, 75.6% of French exports are still concentrated in the European Union and in the three most important non-European, nonemerging markets. China absorbs only 2.8% of French exports (11.1 billion euros) and still represents a smaller export market than that of tiny Switzerland (11.4 billion).

In 2010, France's four main export partners were, in order: Germany, Italy, Belgium and Spain.

Italy. In 2010, Italy traded 337.4 billion euros worth of exports, presenting a trade deficit of 28.6 billion. Exports to E.U. countries totaled 193.2 billion, while exports to the United States, Switzerland, and the OPEC countries amounted to 54.2 billion. In total, the European Union and the three most important non-European, nonemerging markets still represent around 73% of all Italian exports. As in the case of France, in 2010 Italy exported more to Switzerland (16 billion dollars) than to China (8.6 billion).

In 2010, Italy's four main trade partners were, in order, Germany, France, the United States and Spain.

United Kingdom. In 2010, the United Kingdom's exports totaled 306 billion euros with a trade deficit of 117.4 billion.

The European Union represented 53.9% of United Kingdom export destinations, while the United States, Switzerland and OPEC countries made up another 19.5% of British exports. In total, 73.3% of British exports were concentrated within the European Union and the three top non-European, non-emerging markets. China absorbs only 2.7% of United Kingdom exports (that is, 8.3 billion euros) and it is still by far the United Kingdom's least important trade partner, falling behind Ireland with 19.1 billion.

In 2010, the United Kingdom's four main trade partners were, in order, the United States, Germany, the Netherlands and France.

Appendix 10

The Financial Interdependencies Between the Banking Systems of the Six Main European Countries with Regard to the Economies of Other Countries

The growing interrelations between the different European national banking systems and the numerous activities carried out by respective economic systems in other partner countries have created strong interdependencies in terms of interlinked foreign bank exposures. This is what Table 1 demonstrates, summarizing the consolidated credits of the banking systems of each of the main E.U. countries (Germany, France, the United Kingdom, Italy, the Netherlands and Spain) in relation to the economies of each of the other five partner countries at the end of March 2011. The main fact that emerges from the table is the large exposure in absolute value of banking systems of the three biggest E.U. countries (Germany, France and the United Kingdom) to the other five countries considered: the exposure of the French banking system to Germany, the United Kingdom, Italy, the Netherlands and Spain at the end of March 2011 amounted to a total of 1.253 trillion dollars; the total exposure of the German banking system to the other five countries was 1.237 trillion dollars; that of the UK banking system was 790 billion.

Countries of the lending banks	Borrowing countries						Total
	GE	FR	UK	IT	NL	ES	
GE		207	520	165	167	178	1,237
FR	266		295	410	136	146	1,253
UK	192	294		69	134	101	790
IT	272	43	48		26	32	420
NL	193	85	107	49		76	511
SP	59	30	430	36	19		573

Table 1. Reciprocal interdependencies of the banking systems of the six main E.U. countries in terms of foreign exposure: absolute value (in billions of dollars). Consolidated credit of the banking systems abroad, ultimate risk basis, stock at the end of March 2011. (Source: Bank for International Settlements)

Spain, the Netherlands and Italy follow at a distance, with a total exposure in absolute value to the other five main E.U. partner countries of, respectively: 573,511 and 420 billion dollars.

France, Germany and the United Kingdom are also the countries that display the strongest reciprocal interrelations.

The consolidated credit of Germany toward the UK amounts to 520 billion dollars, toward France 207, making a total of 727 billion with the two partner countries.

The consolidated credit of France toward Germany and the United Kingdom comes to a total of 561 billion dollars (295 to the United Kingdom and 266 to Germany), while the United Kingdom's credit toward Germany and France reaches 486 billion dollars (of which 192 billion to Germany and 294 to France).

As far as Italy is concerned, we can observe that, on the one hand it is mostly exposed to Germany (272 billion dollars) and on the other hand, it is the country to which France is most exposed, with 410 billion dollars of consolidated credit. The Netherlands is exposed to Germany most of all (193 billion dollars), and Spain is most exposed to the United Kingdom (430 billion).

Countries of the lending banks	Borrowing countries						Total
	GE	FR	UK	IT	NL	SP	
GE		5.9	14.8	4.7	4.8	5.1	35.1
FR	9.7		10.8	14.9	4.9	5.3	45.6
UK	7.9	12.2		2.9	5.5	4.2	32.7
IT	12.4	1.9	2.2		1.2	1.4	19.1
NL	23.1	10.2	12.8	5.9		9.1	61.1
SP	3.9	2.0	28.5	2.4	1.2		38.0

Table 2. Reciprocal interdependencies of the banking systems of six main E.U. countries in terms of foreign exposure: in % of GDP of the lending countries (2010). Consolidated credit of banking systems to foreign countries, ultimate risk basis, stock at the end of March 2011. (Source: Bank for International Settlements)

It is interesting, in order to have a basis of comparison for the data, to also evaluate the extent of the banking exposure of each of the countries to the other main partners in percentages of their own GDP. Table 2 takes the GDPs of 2010 as a reference point and shows the total exposure of the Dutch banking system in the other five main E.U. countries totaled 61.1% of its own GDP. Other countries with a very high exposure in relation to GDP include France (45.6%); Spain (38%) and (Germany 35.1%). Italy however stands out as having a very minor proportion of its GDP exposed to the other five main E.U. partner countries, only 19.1%.

In recent years a new and remarkable exposure has emerged: that of the five main European countries (the six listed above with the exception of Spain) to the peripheral countries of the eurozone (Spain, Ireland, Portugal and Greece).

Countries of the lending banks	Borrowing countries				Total four "peripheral" countries
	SP	IE	PT	GR	
GE	178	117	39	24	357
FR	146	30	28	57	261
UK	101	137	27	15	279
NL	76	19	7	5	107
IT	32	13	4	5	54

Table 3. Exposure of the banks of the main E.U. countries to the peripheral eurozone countries: absolute value (in billions of dollars). Consolidated credits of banking systems to foreign countries, ultimate risk basis, stock at the end of March 2011. (Source: Bank for International Settlements)

As Table 3 shows, Germany, the United Kingdom, and France are the countries with the banking systems that are most exposed to the peripheral countries, with a total consolidated credit of 357,279 and 261 billion dollars respectively. The banking systems most exposed to Greece are the French one (57 billion dollars) and the German one (24 billion dollars) while the British banking system, along with the German one, is the most exposed to Ireland (137 and 117 billion respectively). Italy is the country least exposed to the four peripheral countries (54 billion dollars) and to Greece in particular (only 5 billion).

Countries of the lending banks	Borrowing countries				Total four "peripheral" countries
	SP	IE	PT	GR	
GE	5.1	3.3	1.1	0.7	10.1
FR	5.3	1.1	1.0	2.1	9.5
UK	4.2	5.7	1.1	0.6	11.5
NL	9.1	2.2	0.8	0.6	12.8
IT	1.4	0.6	0.2	0.2	2.5

Table 4. The exposure of the banks of the main E.U. countries to the peripheral countries of the eurozone in % of GDP of the lending countries (2010). Consolidated credit of the banking systems, ultimate risk basis, stock at the end of March 2011. (Source: Bank for International Settlements)

As Table 4 shows, the amount of exposure of the Italian banking system to the peripheral countries, expressed in percentage of GDP, is far smaller than that of the other lending countries, just 2.5%, compared with France's 9.5%, Germany's 10.1%, the United Kingdom's 11.5% and the Netherlands' 12.8%.

Appendix 11

Three Intervention Mistakes After Deauville

In the year following Deauville, three ill-advised mistakes were made, and they continue to be made today:

a) The first mistake was the spontaneous and meddling decision made by the ECB—spontaneous and meddling depending on the degree of analytical hypocrisy that one applies to the situation. This was the mistake of thinking that the intervention of the ECB in the so-called secondary market, the acquisition of bonds from states in crisis, was enough. You will remember that in May 2010 acquisition on the secondary market on the part of the ECB was one of the forecasted interventions. But not the only one. There was also at that time a reliance on the timely and coordinated activation of all the other instruments: from the EFSF, to the European semester and the common budget policy.

What is important is that the intervention on the so-called secondary market was aimed at old bonds, already present on the market after having been issued by the states, and so permitted by treaties. Given that the boundary between primary and secondary is effectively opaque, it should still be noted that this is a distortionary rather than decisive technique. Distortionary because it doesn't stop but rather encourages speculators, given that they thus come to know in advance that there will be a final buyer. It is also distortionary because it can favor the banks that are discreetly chosen by the ECB as privileged counterparties for the disinvestment, handled by the ECB itself, of entire portfolios of the bonds of states in crisis. It is above all distortionary, as we will see shortly, because it influences and/or can influence, from the outside, even without real final ultimate stabilizing effects, the internal policy of an individual state. Finally, it is not decisive because, as the results of these last few months demonstrate, it produces some positive economic effects, but no definitive structural effects. Buying and more buying and nothing happens. The holes opening up in the dike are larger than our fingers, so we can't stop the leak.

b) The second mistake was made first by applying a stress test to European banks, based on the mark to market alignment of public stocks in their portfolios, thus creating and/or highlighting enormous real and/or potential losses in their budgets. This accelerated the crisis, because if one state's banks are doing badly then the states are consequently also doing badly. After the stress test came the attempt to set up the European Financial Stability Fund. The logical terms of the sequence were inverted (i.e., beginning with the stress test and following up with the EFSF and not doing it the other way around), so an additional element of instability was introduced into the system—the opposite of the necessary and expected stability. Not to mention that the EFSF is today so limited, given so little financially and so little flexibility, that it seems more like a derivative typical of the financial market rather than a real and new European institution. It is not by chance but for a reason that in its constitution, the EFSF is referenced, in true privatizing spirit, as "the Company"!

c) The third mistake was made at the G20 at Cannes on November 4 to 5, 2011, a replica of Deauville: the removal of the prohibition of thought, the announcement of the possible exit of a state (Greece) from the euro.

Appendix 12

Speech Given at Villa d'Este in Cernobbio—
Friday, September 7, 2007

I will make a very simple speech. I will use three key words: experience, transparency, repentance.

Experience: I believe I have been involved in a potentially similar situation, if a domestic one. I recall the examination of the Parliament of the Republic of Italy on the question of bonds. My speech was not limited to the penal pathological aspects of Parmalat, but extended to encompass a range of considerations related to what had happened in the world of credit during those years. I recall that I put forward the same questions at European meetings and at the G7, and I also remember several discussions in Washington at the SEC. . . .

What has happened? What is being revealed? I believe it is hard to find historical comparisons, as history never repeats itself exactly down to the last detail. In November of last year I gave an interview during which I spoke of these matters. The newspaper gave it a title describing the risk of a "new 1929." I am still a little shocked by the violence of that title, yet perhaps it was a felix culpa. In a way, after the event, I'm not sure if this crisis is like that of 1929, but it is potentially a crisis with a capital C. I want to give you an example that might seem—how to say it?—simple. All you need to do to understand what is happening is to read the newspapers. If confidence is lacking in the markets, it's as if faith is missing from the Church. Something essential is lacking. It is hard to conceive of a market without confidence. And it is paradoxically the market, which is made up of liquidity, not confidence, that is being rocked. Something is not right.

So, briefly, the two key words: transparency and penitence.

First: There has been a tendency not to speak of these things. That is a mistake. Given the intensity and the scale of this crisis, the earlier and the more one talks, the better. It does not make it worse. Occultism is negative, not positive.

Second: the confession, penitence. As I know well, the global economy lacks a global economic government. However there are authorities that together can create a very simple instrument. I believe that in one week we could draft a criterion for a norm that defines what must go into budgets and what can legally be left out of them . . . above or below the line. . . .

If we truly believe that it is essential to restore confidence, then we must do something—not a petition of principle, or an abstract invocation, but something concrete. . . . To join us . . . is to make a statement that you have those things and that you don't have those toxic things. Those who don't join us will obviously remain outside of the system. In order to enforce a norm of this nature, it is not necessary for a political reality to impose it. It is enough that there be a general consensus on the matter. After which, as after all confessions, there is a choice between paradise, in which we all believe, and hell, which we all want to avoid.

Appendix 13

The Glass-Steagall Act

The key principles of the Glass-Steagall law are these: "To provide for the safer and more effective use of the assets of banks, to regulate interbank control, to prevent the undue diversion of funds into speculative operations and for other purposes." In particular:

Section 3(a) states, "Each Federal reserve bank shall keep itself informed of the general character and amount of the loans and investments of its member banks with a view to ascertaining whether undue use is being made of bank credit for the speculative carrying of or trading in securities, real estate, or commodities, or for any other purpose inconsistent with the maintenance of sound credit conditions; and, in determining whether to grant or refuse advances, rediscounts or other credit accommodations, the Federal reserve bank shall give consideration to such information."

Section 7: "The Federal Reserve Board shall have power to direct any member bank to refrain from further increase of its loans secured by stock or bond collateral for any period up to one year under penalty of suspension of all rediscount privileges at Federal reserve banks."

Section 20: "After one year from the date of the enactment of this Act, no member bank shall be affiliated in any manner described in section 2(b) hereof with any corporation, association, business trust, or other similar organization engaged principally in the issue, flotation, underwriting, public sale, or distribution at wholesale or retail or through syndicate participation of stocks, bonds, debentures, notes, or other securities."

Section 21(a): "After the expiration of one year after the date of enactment of this Act it shall be unlawful:

"For any person, firm, corporation, association, business trust, or other similar organization, engaged in the business of issuing, underwriting, selling, or distributing, at wholesale or retail, or through syndicate participation, stocks, bonds, debentures, notes, or other securities, to engage at the same time to any extent whatever in the business of receiving deposits subject to check or to repayment upon presentation of a passbook, certificate of deposit, or other evidence of debt, or upon request of the depositor . . ."

Section 32: "From and after January 1, 1934, no officer or director of any member bank shall be an officer, director, or manager of any corporation, partnership, or unincorporated association engaged primarily in the business of purchasing, selling, or negotiating securities, and no member bank shall perform the functions of a correspondent bank on behalf of any such individual, partnership, corporation, or unincorporated association and no such individual, partnership, corporation, or unincorporated association shall perform the functions or a correspondent for any member bank or hold on deposit any funds on behalf of any member bank, unless in any such case there is a permit therefore issued by the Federal Reserve Board . . ."

Appendix 14

The Global Legal Standard

What is a global legal standard? During the beginnings of the crisis and in its aftermath, now, we have observed as the negative effects of purely technical methods and pure financial competence unfolded in real time. We need to make the law more complex. If not, all that will prevail will be the organized, planned technical nothingness that is typical of corporations.

In its ideal configuration, the GLS is really an economic constitution that encompasses principles and general rules, necessary to create a new world order suited to the market economy.

It is increasingly necessary that we take such action, to avoid the permanence of and/or return to states of nature, to places with anarchy and societal breakdown. In those areas, the evolution of the capitalist model degenerates into disease, with grave negative collateral effects for the real economy as well as civil society.

From a technical point of view the GLS, as its name suggests, is above all a legal standard, a reference model (or a collection of reference models) that encompasses the kind of content that would normally be regulated.

For this reason, that standard must be global. This qualification is closely intertwined with the notion of the GLS itself. In the global world, a standard is global or it doesn't exist. Precisely because it is global, it has the essential function of aligning law and market, a set of principles and rules, shared and accepted by the international community and able to stand as the legal reference points of the global world.

In these terms, the construction of the GLS can only be carried out with political strong-mindedness.

The absence of politics—indecision—would in fact favor this drift towards the technocratic, based on the mistaken theory of the necessary, automatic neutrality of the market.

Of course, even indecision is a political act: an act of abdication.

But the seriousness of the crisis on the one hand and the new structure of the world on the other, require much more: a decisive, positive and constructive politics.

At this point, let me set down an essential premise, a fundamental initial precision: The GLS' purpose is not to create a new international superbureaucracy that aims to develop parasitically through the typical effect of technocratic hubris.

One objection that the cosmo-pessimist might voice against this project is that it is not feasible: Writing principles and rules for the economy of the second millennium can seem like an enormous task and utopian dream.

In reality, what the GLS needs is a cosmopolitan table of general values and rules, and we don't need to start with a clean slate—much of the work has already been done.

The international and supranational institutions (the OECD, the IMF, the World Bank and the European Union) have already created norms, legal models, sector stands and so forth across wide swaths of the law.

There is therefore a lot of legal material available to construct a common and shared legal platform.

These are materials that now can and must be put together, assembled in a new legal architecture. The deconstruction that the forces of globalization have progressively carried out over the course of the 20th century calls now for the process of institutional reconstruction to begin. Recompiling legal materials that are now scattered and dispersed across a variety of macro and micro systems. The fundamental instrument that's needed to pass from the abstract to the concrete is a multi-lateral international treaty. The most important legal infrastructure that can be adapted to globalization is the international treaty, an international treaty that is open to the adherence of the states.

The first steps have already been taken to introduce the GLS through an ad hoc multilateral international treaty.

The first step is the declaration of so-called PIT principles (propriety, integrity, transparency), approved by the OECD in May 2010, at the behest of Italy.

Declarations such as this one carry a solemn weight and carry political commitments for the member states of the OECD—and for close non-members—even if they are not obligatory in a legal sense.

Such acts can not only pave the way for legal paths applicable within the member states, but also anticipate the development of covenant-like networks between states. These acts are typical of so-called soft law, but lay the groundwork for the incorporation of the GLS in acts of hard law, that is, in a true and proper multilateral international treaty.

In this way, a new multilateral international treaty could be progressively delineated, in the form of a new international code that values decency, transparency and integrity in all economic and financial operations. An international treaty is, I repeat, the legal infrastructure that is the best suited to globalization. It would be the primary symbol of a new order.

This is certainly not a simple process. It is essential that we discuss it and support it, in universities, within economic, social and trade systems and organizations and in circles of civic engagement so that the project progresses and is not abandoned. We need something to convey this permanent political message to the people, a message that is shared and strong because it is based on interests but also and above all on fundamental ethical values.

In any case, it is clear that the impact of GLS would not be limited to the economic world, as it would also serve to protect social rights. It is for this reason that the GLS can be a solid platform, if not for de-globalization then certainly for the redesign and rebalancing of its effects. The effects of globalization have been so far positive for multinational capital, which has de-localized production in search of commercial outlets and above all in search of low-cost work forces, and also for financial capital, which has found in globalization a way to create its own enormous if ephemeral fortune.

These have been advantageous effects, to the detriment of the proportion of the workforce that has remained in its traditional place and that now finds salaries as well as social rights reduced or capped, a harbinger of poverty.[25] For this reason, too, in order to fend off such poverty, the GLS is essential.

[25] G. Tremonti, *The Ghost of Poverty*, 1995.